A Single
DIVA's
Guide

to
The Science of Attracting Love!

by Shay 'Your Love DIVA'

Shay Better Publishing

Alpharetta, Georgia

First Printing 2018

ISBN-13: 978-0-9823084-9-3

Shay Better Publishing
4575 Webb Bridge Road, #4996
Alpharetta, Georgia 30005, USA

Printed in the United States of America by Lulu Press

Cover design by Michael Alexandru Dumitru

Editing and Design by Annie Leonard

Dedication

To my daughters,

From a place of wholeness,
may you fearlessly and easily
attract the love God intended for us all!

Contents

Foreword

As a father of a 30-something-year-old daughter who is single and has given up on looking for her soulmate, I am concerned. I don't want my daughter to give up on meeting that perfect young, black man who will respect, love, and hell yeah, worship at her feet, knowing she can do no wrong. I want a man to treat her like a queen, grow old with her, and give her a house full of babies so I can be a proud grandfather one day. My deepest desire is for her to be happy and in love, love, love. I have dreamt about that day when I walk her down the aisle to give her hand in marriage. When we have family dinners or for the holidays, I want to hear the happiness in her voice because he surprised her with flowers. Like most fathers, I want my baby girl to have the best and find a man to treat her like I do.

When my daughter tells me that there are no good black men and she has given up on ever finding love, I can see in her eyes that deep down inside she still hopes to find "him," and I do too. I don't want her to be the favorite single aunt or the old maid who all the other grandchildren go to for cookies and milk. I can't see her not having children because she would make a great mother. Although I don't want to see her alone, I don't want her to just have any man for the sake of having a man. I don't want a man to look at her as a sugar mama, a female ATM, or a sister who will settle for anything he throws at her. Thankfully, she is not desperate, and furthermore, I don't want to have to do time in prison because I had to shoot a brother for disrespecting my baby.

This book will give her and many women who have dads like me hope that they will find love, a real, lasting love. When I first read this manuscript, I called 10 of my girlfriends and told them that I was reading a book that will change their lives. All of them are single and looking. I have witnessed them abase men to the point where I had to leave the room. At other times, we have had many hours of

1

conversations about men and male issues, including why men cheat, are all the good men gay, and is there a man left without baby mama drama. Many of these women have libraries of "how to find a man" books and magazines with advice columns on the subject. This book, however, is going to become their "bible." In fact, this book will become the bible for women of all nationalities, ages or status.

I truly commend Shay for sharing her personal story and expertise, and I am excited that she asked me to put my voice in this book.

J L King
New York Times Best-Selling Author

P.S. My personal message to every woman who reads this book is to always practice safe sex, and don't give away your power of choice. Keep in mind, every man you meet might have a secret, and you should take your time to get to know him in and out of the bed.

Preface

This is the 3rd edition of this book. It was my goal to change the energy and focus from avoiding 'getting played' to attracting your 'perfect partner'. The first edition was a source of healing for me. I was angry and in a lot of pain, and I wanted to teach other women how to avoid experiencing that pain. I'm afraid that my pain and fear may have come through in my original writing. I revised the book as my energy changed, but in the 2nd edition I was still trying to figure it out and was still on a path to healing childhood issues that caused me to attract the worst kind of men. Many read that edition and thought that I had lost my mind. I had lost my mind somewhere between Peachtree Street and the corner of Atlanta Highway! I write this version after years of healing, prayer, and reaching a place of wholeness. I write this book after enjoying four happy years of marriage with my God-sent soulmate.

In writing this book, I wanted to tell my story and provide the lessons I took away from my experiences in order to give single women and women with children a comprehensive dating and relationship guide. I offer this guide with a combination of old-school rules and law-of-attraction principles. I know that a love exists for you that can be magical if you are able to unlock the unknown and trust that better is waiting for you. The advice I give is a dose of tough love from a sister-girlfriend figure. My advice is meant to improve you as a person – not just for attracting a mate but to attract all that you wish for in life. My goal is to always reach you in a way that you have never been reached before and to awaken in you a better way of dating and interacting with men. This requires me to be more concerned about the way you feel about yourself and to help you discover what unresolved issues still linger within you. This also requires that I be direct and upfront with you. The words or phrases I use may shock you. I do this on purpose using Neuro-linguistic programming to help invoke a change in your thinking and behavior. You will get mad at me (yourself) from time to time but know that everything I say is spoken with so much love and for the purpose of getting you past your limitations. Once I am able to help you believe that you deserve love and that something better awaits you, transforming you into an irresistible DIVA is the easy part.

How am I able to offer such advice, you ask? The best people to take advice from are the ones who have the scars to prove they went through something, learned the lessons, and survived. I have my scars, a ton of them, and I will share all my bumps and bruises with you and the lessons I have learned. My journey of figuring out the self-defeating behavior that caused my constant failures in relationships started after my divorce in 2005, when I began a relationship with a man I cared for deeply and made just about every mistake a woman can make in dating. Here is a short list of my mistakes: having sex too soon, accepting his lies, pursuing him once he started losing interest in me, making excuses for his disrespectful behavior that clearly demonstrated that he was just not feeling me anymore, and accepting so many other behaviors that showed that he was a Don't Wanter (Chapter 5).

Needless to say, we did not work out, but there was a blessing in the lesson! He taught me that I had lots to learn about men and dating. Therefore, I decided to immerse myself in learning all that I could about what I did wrong. I launched and completed an initiative to date 100 men in six months. I have to say, the journey was entertaining and insightful. To add to my research, I spoke to countless single, dating men and women, and even interviewed happily married older couples, some of whom had children before the men entered the picture. My goal of understanding men, relationships, and my own inadequacies led to my writing this guide.

I now have a *YouTube* channel at *www.youtube.com/lovein30days* that has grown in popularity. On my show, I offer free advice to women on the common issues encountered in love, dating, and relationships. I also have a coaching practice in which I coach professional singles searching for healthy relationships and who desire to get married.

With all my mistakes, experiences, and discoveries from the experiences of others, I have published three books and several articles in major magazines and lectured all over the world teaching women how to gain a competitive advantage in the world of dating. I have appeared on radio shows, done TV appearances, and participated in public roundtable discussions on the topics of love, dating, and relationships. In doing this, I have discovered that each "expert" has his or her own theories on what works in these areas, but very few can apply scientific facts to these opinions. This is where I come in. As a pre-medicine biology major, who is also a top-performing pharmaceutical sales representative, knowing and explaining the science behind human behavior is important to me. I have removed my personal, female opinions and feelings and have created products based on the feedback of over 3,000 men, women, and happy couples. I have also tested this knowledge and received TONS of testimonials from people I have helped all around the world. I have learned a lot through my *YouTube* videos by interacting with everyday people experiencing dating challenges that are common everywhere, and it is my accessibility, science, and law-of-attraction-based approach to relationship advice that sets me apart from so many relationship authors and experts.

In addition, I am happily married after having been proposed to by at least seven different men and married and divorced 1.3 times. I will explain the .3 later. I know what you're thinking. Why the heck would you take advice from someone who has failed at relationships so badly? I am the last person you should take advice from, right?

No, wrong! My past mistakes work in your favor. How many single women do you know who are over 40 and have never been proposed to - let alone married? I have had lots of great guys fall for me, but until I could get past my limitations, I could not 'see' them. I may have made poor choices in the dating game, but I got it at least 60% right before I figured out how to get it 100% right and found my soul mate who happened to also be my childhood sweetheart and first love. I not only mastered how to attract a man but also how to get a man to marry me. I am the perfect coach because I have been where you are, know your challenges, and know the path to attracting a healthy relationship. For example, if I have been overweight most of my life and desire to hire a trainer to assist me with losing weight, I don't want the really skinny trainer who has been skinny all her life and doesn't have a clue as to how or why I can't seem to lose weight. I want the trainer who has been through some weight loss challenges of her own, overcame them, and has been able to maintain a healthy weight. I want her to use her past struggle and failures to help me get over my hurdles.

My love fails can help you avoid the same pitfalls or at least provide a road map out. I failed my way to true love and was brave enough not to quit no matter how much it hurt along the way. I can help guide you to your true love with my bumps as a guide.

I have not only written and published three books, I have also created a non-profit organization called DIVA WISDOM (Women Inspired to Successfully Date Only for Marriage) to help prevent and end single parenting and teen pregnancy by educating and encouraging women to make wise relationship choices and to remain open to new and healthy relationships that ultimately lead to marriage.

I also opened an online university to help coach women to become the type of woman who can attract her husband and go on to maintain a healthy relationship. The point of all of this is to have my finger on the pulse of the issues most people encounter in love, dating, and relationships and continue to come up with innovative ways to solve those problems.

I may have written the words on the pages of this book, but there have been people in my life without whom I may not have accomplished this goal. I am thankful first to Papa God for blessing and keeping me through the storm, for there were many visible and invisible forces that tried to stand in the way of this message getting out to women. I also thank my loving husband and best friend, 'My Carly', who loved me back to life and accepts me, flaws and all. He is the one constant in my life and I thank God for him. I send pure light and love to my children, church family, and closest friends. I will always be thankful to God for them.

Shay Levister

♥

Introduction

As you read this, you are probably asking, "How is this dating guide so different from other dating or relationship books?"

Well, let me start by answering that question. Many dating books on the market today tell women how to think like a man, date like a man, and fall in love with a man. Others claim to inform you how to get your man to commit, or even better, how to get your man to marry you. The difference between those dating books and this guide is that this one offers a little of that while also offering scientifically proven, extensively researched information that has successfully helped hundreds of women. The difference between this book and the hundreds of relationship books on the market is that I combine science (the why), dating rules (the how to), and Law of Attraction/spiritual principles (the power). In addition, it's the only comprehensive guide on the market for single mothers navigating the dating process.

You will discover secrets about men that will make you so irresistible, your new problem will be deciding which men to accept dates with every weekend. If you have been out of the dating game for a while, this guide will teach you how to re-enter the dating world as a more refined you. It will also teach you how to date as a single woman or as a single woman with kids instead of a "single mom" and avoid the pitfalls many women make while dating. It will teach you how to understand the psychology of a man and how to use this knowledge to your advantage. It will teach you which men to avoid, where to go to meet men, and how to distinguish the good ones from the bad.

This book will teach you how to date, make a good impression, and get a second, third, and fourth date – hopefully, leading to a beautiful relationship and ultimately marriage. It will teach you how to think as a desirable woman does and what to do in the relationship so that the man keeps coming back for more. This guide works for any woman despite her looks, background, or number of children!

Single Women with Children

If you are a single mother, your dynamic is very different from that of a single woman with no kids, which makes the dating game much more difficult for you. You are busy, often tired from working to support your children, and cautious about the man you will bring into your children's lives. For this reason, you must understand the dating game and put forth your best in order to attract the right man for you and your children. Keep in mind this guide is not going to tell you to hunt for a father for your kids. Nor will it instruct you to hunt for someone to help take care of your day-to-day responsibilities (i.e., paying your bills). It will simply help you open up to finding the perfect partner for you, a man who will love, cherish, and respect you, and ultimately offer the same to your children.

I was a divorced single woman with two small children. After my divorce, I entered several relationships with men I cared for deeply and made just about every mistake a woman can make in the dating world. I will do my best to be fully transparent with you in the hopes that my past can bring you healing and love.

Throughout this book, I will get very personal with you and share my experiences and mistakes to drive home the point that you are not damaged goods. You are NOT far from transforming your love life into an experience you desire and deserve. As a now happily-married woman, I continue to learn from my mistakes and write them down so that in the future I can bring you advice to help you maintain and improve your future marriage. This is a never-ending journey of the good and the bad with the understanding that the beauty of love is well worth it.

❤

You are almost there. The rest of your life begins in just a few short sentences.

Once you are armed with the understanding of how to date as a DIVA (Divine, Intelligent, Vivacious, Alluring), you will be on your way to more quality men, more options, and ultimately, more satisfying relationships.

Using this Book

Here are some items you may need while reading this book:

- Journal or Notebook
- Poster board
- Candles and Matches
- Magazines
- Scissors
- Glue

You can read this book alone or with a group of other single women. For those who want to complete this book with a friend or group, here are some suggestions.

DIVA Love Buddy

A DIVA Love Buddy is like a workout buddy in a gym. Buddies remind you of your goals and keep you on track toward your desired goal or destiny. They follow up with you on a consistent basis and make sure that you are doing your journaling exercises and affirmations. The buddy process should help you learn how to let go and become vulnerable. You cannot receive love if you are unable to be vulnerable with another person. Being successfully married to your soulmate requires that you allow yourself to let go and completely trust someone other than yourself. If you cannot even trust a stranger or someone with whom you will not be intimate, you will be unable to trust and let go with your husband (more about this later).

When you start to develop feelings for one of the men you are dating, because you will be dating three at a time (I will explain later), your buddy will need to meet that person and be able to give you their honest opinion. This will help you remove the rose-colored glasses and see the man you are dating for who he really is. Your partner will know your goals, objectives, and past dating mistakes, so she can help you avoid the same mistakes when she sees you heading in that direction.

DIVA-in-Training Group

A DIVA-in-Training Group is a group of women on the path toward attracting a healthy love experience using my advice. The group will meet weekly or bi-monthly and discuss topics and lessons shared in the "Attract the Mate" program (Can be found at *www.ShayBetter.com*. The benefit of working within a group is that you will be accountable to the group and your DIVA Love Buddy. This will help to increase your success rate for completing your journey to love and doing what it takes to get over your barriers and attract the love you desire. When that fool of an ex pops back up in your life, just knowing that you will have to report or share your slip up with the group will make you more likely to turn him down and move on toward better. When you meet a man who refuses to take you out or over his place, your DIVA Love Buddy and group will tell you the truth you are afraid to admit to yourself. They will tell you that the man is probably married, taken, or not worth your time.

The purpose of the group is not to get together each week and complain about how there are not enough good men out there. The goal of the group is to keep each other focused and optimistic. You will find that your success rate flies through the roof when you are a part of a collective group doing the meditations together, learning and growing together, and desiring the best love experience for each participant of the group.

> *"Love is passion, obsession, someone you can't live without. If you don't start with that, what are you going to*

end up with? Fall head over heels. I say find someone you can love like crazy and who'll love you the same way back. And how do you find him? Forget your head and listen to your heart. I'm not hearing any heart. Run the risk, if you get hurt, you'll come back. Because, the truth is there is no sense living your life without this. To make the journey and not fall deeply in love - well, you haven't lived a life at all. You have to try. Because if you haven't tried, you haven't lived."

William Parrish
in *Meet Joe Black*

The Process

After my divorce, I didn't think I would find my soulmate at all. For the first year after my divorce, no man approached me or asked me out on a date.

Not one flirted with me or even looked my way. I assumed that it was because I had lost my swagger after being married for several years and was no longer appealing to the opposite sex. It did not bother me one way or the other because I had given up on men and was committed to being happy on my own. However, this was an unrealistic mindset because although I was happy, I still felt that something was missing from my life. Instinctively, I craved being with and being loved by a man. No matter what I tried to tell others and myself, this feeling did not go away.

It was not until I ran into an old high school friend that I discovered that it was not my lack of appeal that kept men at bay. He told me that the reason men had not approached me was because I was sending a nonverbal message that said: "Stay away," and "I am not interested!" As a result, men did just that; they stayed away. This was a wake-up call for me to change my attitude about and toward men.

As I stated earlier, in the beginning of my dating process, I made lots of mistakes and continued to experience disappointment after disappointment. Still, something in me told me to not give up. Something in me also said that there was something I did not know about men, dating, and relationships that I needed to learn quickly if I was to ever find what I truly desired.

After I graduated from the school of hard knocks and completed my dating research, I discovered that attracting a man was so easy that I could set my watch by it. I learned that it was about how I behaved and spoke and what I said while on dates. I discovered that my mindset changed as I transformed into a DIVA! I began to experiment with my newfound power and teach others the same secrets I had learned. The techniques never failed, and I found that I was able to capture the heart of almost any man that I chose.

The catch is that although I can teach you how to attract a man with simply learning and understanding the psychology of a man, the problem is the type of man you would attract. I don't want you to catch a man just to say that you've found one. I want you to attract a good man and keep him!

The point is, yes, I promise you that it is very realistic to attract the man of your dreams if you follow the key advice that I give. It is also realistic to attract a great man in a short period of time if you believe you can and if you are truly ready for the process. I never said that you would fall in love in 30 days, and I discourage anyone from rushing the process of love. If you are ready and BELIEVE that you will attract your soul mate now, follow the advice shared in this book. You may very well meet him in 30 days, but then you will need to give that relationship the time it needs to grow into a love experience. I look at finding love like going fishing. You can catch a fish in 15 minutes if you use the right bait, remain still, and know when to pull up after you have received a good catch. But it will take a little more time and process before you can eat and really enjoy that fish. You must take the fish home, clean it, season it, and cook it. Several hours later, you would have a well-prepared feast worth the process you endured to enjoy it. A relationship is the same way. Learn how to attract the right man without taking a lifetime to do it; but once you have found a potential life partner, give the process time to bring forth a wonderful demonstration of love that you can enjoy for a lifetime.

Many of you still do not believe you can attract the man of your dreams. The truth is if you do NOT believe that you can and do not trust that he has been divinely created just for you, well then, you are right! Your journey to attracting the man of your dreams starts when you are ready.

Begin by evaluating yourself emotionally, financially, spiritually, and mentally; and make a choice as to whether you are ready for the man of your dreams to walk into your life. Be honest with yourself. Sometimes, all it takes is 30 days to focus on you, love who you truly are, and accept your current situation in order to be ready to find the man of your dreams. Sometimes it takes longer.

For myself, I took six months to pray, meditate, get my credit straightened out, my business and finances in order, and mentally get it together. I understood that I must become what I wanted to attract and that I needed to give myself time and space to do this. When I was done, I was mentally, emotionally, and spiritually ready to accept the idea of finding the man of my dreams. I dated several men, did everything I teach in this book, and to my delight, I found my soulmate! He is everything I have ever wanted in a man. He is kind, strong, caring, nurturing, and a true king. He loves me with all of him and does not allow me to refer to the kids as "my kids." He loves me so much that he took on the responsibility of being daddy to my two children and loves them dearly. He does not mind being the provider and protector, and he supports my dreams and goals. I am so thankful to God for bringing him to me and allowing me to 'see' him.

My husband and I were high school sweethearts who met when we were 14 years old. We stayed friends through college and while he served in the Air Force. I still have the letters he wrote me. When I graduated from college, he left the Air Force and moved to Atlanta with the expectation that he was coming home to me and that we could finally be together. I didn't get the memo. When he called after several months of losing contact, my ex answered the phone and never told me that my friend called. My husband-to-be was so heartbroken that he walked away and didn't try to call again. Seven years later we bumped into each other in the most serendipitous way and became close friends again. His feelings for me, he shared, never wavered, but I friend-zoned him and wasn't ready for my 'good guy' yet. After dating a few jerks and experiencing further dating disappointments, one day God opened my eyes and revealed that he was my life partner. The irony is that at the same moment we both called each other to reveal our feelings for each other and that we didn't want to ever lose our 'friend'. We have been together since that day.

But there were many days before that when I wanted to give up hope.

Some days I cried and prayed for God to send me my soulmate. No matter how bad it got or how many 'dates' or relationships did not work out, I maintained the faith. I knew I would attract him.

I share this to say that if you are hurting emotionally, or some portions of your life seem to be out of order, then you are not ready to begin your journey of attracting the man of your dreams.

Close this book, breathe, and give yourself space and time to actively allow yourself to heal and completely repair these areas of your life. Read Chapter 1 and Chapter 2 and focus on the advice that talks about healing and getting over your issues.

However, if you already believe that you can and will attract the man of your dreams, that you are ready to be completely satisfied with where you are in your life, and are willing to follow the advice in this guide, then you are ready to begin your journey with me towards attracting a life partner who will rock your world in every sense of the word!

Chapter 1.
Getting Over Your Barriers

My aunt yelled, "You ain't worth shit. You're the reason why your daddy couldn't be a father to his other children and why they never had a father!" My father, two half-sisters, a half-brother and uncle sat and watched as my aunt spewed her venom, which tore into my heart.

Six hours earlier, I'd arrived in New York dreading the idea of being around these people I called family. I was a sophomore in college at the time and was in New York to attend the funeral of my 22-year-old cousin who'd died of kidney disease.

I was all grown up, and in my mind, my family could no longer hurt me with their negativity and hatred. However, what I didn't realize was that I subconsciously believed what they said and how they felt about me. This belief fueled the self-hatred that allowed me to accept and attract being mistreated not only by lovers, but by people in general.

A male cousin picked me up from the airport and took me directly to the viewing of my cousin's body. My plane had been delayed so we were rushing to get to the viewing on time. I was not looking forward to seeing a dead body for the first time in my life, let alone that of my sweet cousin who had died too soon. Without thinking about where I was, I decided to leave my things in the car, including my luggage, journals, and my college sweetheart's jacket, which was sentimental to him because it was given to him by his big sister whom he was really close to.

I was wearing my sharpest white suit and my (false) confidence was high. I only wanted to see and speak to a handful of people because I'd decided that I did not give two cents what anyone thought about me. I was no longer the little girl who would tolerate getting put down by her father's side of the family. My paternal grandmother could not force me to eat anymore of her over-seasoned cooking, and my half siblings could not make me feel less than them because I spoke with a southern drawl while they maintained their strong New York accent.

I was angry, bitter, and immaturely naive to the reality and what I was attracting. To make matters worse, luck just wasn't on my side. When I went outside to retrieve my things from my cousin's car, I discovered that someone else had gotten to them sooner. I was robbed!

After crying and making the necessary phone calls, I went upstairs to join the family meeting. Soon enough, I realized that I did not walk into a meeting; I walked into an ambush!

At this point, my aunt was in my face, "That's right, you high yellow bitch," she yelled. "It's your fault why your siblings hate you so much! You have always been spoiled and selfish and only care about you damn self! Why I ought to whoop your ass right now!"

Several things went through my mind before a family member jumped in to defuse the situation. The one thing that stood out to me the most was that my father just sat there and didn't even try to protect me.

This had not been the first time my father didn't protect me when I thought that he should have. This experience was nothing compared to my first wedding when my father stood me up. Although I knew my dad probably wouldn't keep his promise to be there, I demanded that my wedding to my first husband be delayed another 30 minutes as I stood out in the hot sun sweating, crying, and waiting for my daddy to show up.

♥

For years I blamed my father for my dysfunctional relationships, my pain, and my anger. I later learned from Tony Robbins, the world-famous life coach and strategist, whose seminars I credit for many of my life changes, that if you blame someone significant in your life for the bad, you have to blame them for the good too. If it were not for my father, I would have never desired love so badly that nothing could have stopped me from finding it. He taught me how to be strong, put education first, and aim for excellence. Most importantly, he gave me the perfect picture of exactly what I did not want to end up with in a husband.

There is a long history behind my father's actions that explain why generational pain continued to flow through the veins of each member of my family, including me. It had not completely sunk in at this time that my father was incapable of giving me more than he gave. He was a self-proclaimed loner who cared very deeply for himself and about what other people thought about him. He was a prideful, hard-working West Indian man who owned a heating and air conditioning business, loved cookies and ice cream for dinner, and could throw the worst temper tantrum this side of heaven. My father was a make-it-happen kind of man who always found a way to get what he wanted. He never accepted "no" for an answer and prided himself on being able to live an upper-middle class lifestyle in a Caucasian neighborhood.

With more than ten children by the age of 60, he was definitely a lady's man who did not believe in contraception. It was his culture that women were to be conquered and dominated; that the darker you are, the harder life would be for you; and that love was something that hurt and was conditional.

"Red face" was the nickname he gave me, and there was no doubt in anyone's mind growing up that I was 'daddy's girl.' I grew up hearing that he married my light complexioned, African American and German Jew mixed-heritage mother so that I would come out light-skinned. My father told me almost daily that no man would ever want me if I got too fat. This led me to believe my value lay in my outer appearance.

It was at this moment, while standing in the hallway of my uncle's home after the wake, that I decided I would never marry a man like him. Unfortunately, it was at that moment I also set into motion attracting many men like him. I was 19 years old and too immature to realize that my father did the best with what he knew. I was too hurt to see that hurt people hurt people, and that his pain restricted him from loving me the way I craved to be loved. I didn't see then that my father's dysfunction was fueled by his own pain and fears. All I could see and feel was my resentment for him resulting from all his broken promises, verbal abuse, and the physical abuse of my brother and mother.

Your False Beliefs

It wasn't always this way between my father and I. Up until the age of 14, I adored my daddy and worshipped the ground he walked on. I mean it. He was like Jesus to me. I felt he could do no wrong and there wasn't anything that he did not know. Every night when he came home, I would run into his arms and he would hug me and do a dance as he sang me a special song. We would dance and dance until he got tired.

Sometimes we would stay up all night long as I sat on his lap while watching Michael Jackson videos. I loved my dad so much and believed that he was perfect in every way – except when he was abusive toward my mother and brother because they did something he disliked or when he shouted profanities throughout the house.

My vision of my dad utterly shattered the day he was caught having one of many rumored extramarital affairs. When I grew old enough to see and acknowledge his imperfections, my heartbreak cycle started.

♥

After years of residual pain, I grew to resent my father and saw all men as a reflection, in some way, of my dad. I was attractive, smart, outgoing, and successful at everything I did, but I continued to sabotage great relationships and gravitated towards men who were emotionally unavailable to love me. With all my supposed beauty, I consistently kept getting hurt as I was left feeling like I was not good enough for any man's love.

This pain eventually started to affect my professional life – every aspect of our lives is interconnected. In my younger years, I would get a job with my amazing drive and talent only to lose it because deep down inside I did not like myself, so I sabotaged anything good that came to me. I knew it was my bitterness and resentment that affected me because I became angry and rebellious toward authority figures. It wasn't until I watched the movie "Seabiscuit" and saw the part when the jockey lost a race because he would rather fight the person who fouled him rather than focus on winning the race, that I realized I was still angry at my dad and resisting leadership and men because it reminded me of my dad's controlling behavior and abuse.

One day, I had enough and decided to forgive my father and all those who had injured me, so I could attract better experiences into my life. I also read the book *Calling in The One* by Katherine Woodward Thomas. I swear by this book as a tool to help with your journey to self-healing, which is necessary before attracting The One into your life. I performed healing rituals, which I will share, and repeated daily affirmations to help transform my life.

The people who show up in your life reflect the way you feel about yourself; and until you heal your false beliefs about yourself, you will always attract people who confirm your own self-hatred. You will see through the stories of my relationships that really, I hated myself and believed that I was not deserving of a healthy love experience. I grew up feeling as though I had to earn my father's love, so I approached all my relationships in this manner and ended up hurt every time. Many of you share the same daddy issues I had and are consistently coming up with the short end of the stick in love, dating, and relationships.

Remember, no matter what you have been through or how much you feel you do not deserve love, being loved in a healthy, unconditional manner is your birthright. You are worthy of attracting someone who loves, honors, and respects you and this is a reality you must accept in order to attract that experience.

By recognizing the limiting beliefs standing in the way of allowing true love to walk through your door, you become empowered to think and do something different which will lead to a different outcome.

Healing from Rape

Studies show that 1 out of every 3 women have been sexually violated at some point in their lives. At least 90% of the women that I coach have been molested or sexually violated in some way. The sense of invasion leaves lasting effects that will go on to affect the way she interacts with men until she is able to heal the trauma of being raped. Many women who are very promiscuous or seek attention through sexual means or by dressing provocatively were raped by a father, uncle, ex-boyfriend, or a stranger. Within these women is a festering sore filled with the puss of rage, loss, sometimes self-blame, and confusion. An innocence was stolen, and a void left in its place that victims often attempt to fill with empty, emotionless sex and attention.

Whether the rape occurred when she was a child or an adult, the trauma is still severe. It is further amplified if the assaults happened over a period of time and the adults around the child didn't believe them, ignored it, or neglected to protect the child in the first place by leaving them with a pervert who violated the mother when she was a child or violated someone else the adults knew. The abuse becomes a sick secret that carries generational pain within many families who ignore the perverted uncle who is known to inappropriately touch girls or who has been accused of sexual molestation or rape. This pattern must stop with you, the reader, if you were the victim. It was not your fault and there is nothing you "should have done" to prevent it from happening. Know that in your heart and mind that you can and will heal if you work at it.

The energy of rape is so heavy that it buries itself deeply within every cell in one's body. As a spiritual reader and healer, I can almost always feel when a woman has been violated. I can even 'see' it in the beginning of a telephone coaching session. It is for this reason that healing must take place emotionally, subconsciously, and spiritually. This healing will remove the debris and soul tie created from the rape experience.

If you have been sexually violated in any way, you must heal the trauma of this experience before you can attract a healthy relationship. Listen to the Inner Child and Healing Rape Trauma meditation in order to heal on multiple layers from that experience.

Unlike when you were a child, you now have the power to control what happens to you. You have the power to change your story and take back your power from the person who took it from you. They do not deserve you spending your entire life alone or in messed up relationships. Decide now that they cannot have your right to be loved unconditionally by a good man. It will take work. You may need coaching. Either way, commit to yourself that your story begins on your terms and that you will do whatever it takes to heal, break the cycle, and attract your soulmate to you.

Your Exes

Many single women, whether they have been married or not, are emotionally injured by the men in their past. As a result, many of you are walking around with memories of lost relationships and the pain from those relationships still etched in your heart. For some of you, it has been years since you have dated because you no longer trust men and are unwilling to take the risk of being burned by love again. Even more of you hold mottos like: "I can do bad all by myself" and "To hell with men; who needs them!" The answer to the latter statement is: you do!

After you have finished rolling your eyes and declaring with your finger in the air, "I don't need a man in my life," please pay attention as I say this in slow motion: If you do not need a man in your life, then why, oh why are you reading this guide? Why do you look at happy couples holding hands and say to yourself, why don't I have that? Why do you detest being around your happily married friends when they are with their husbands? It's because a) you are not asexual, and b) God in Her infinite wisdom, understood that if She did not place that yearning to be with a man inside of you, then the human species would have become extinct long ago.

It is natural to want to be with someone special who loves and cherishes only you and who looks forward to coming home to only you. Someone you can talk to when you are down and who shares in your victories as well. Love makes life so fascinating, fulfilling, and enriching. No matter how many times you have been hurt or disappointed by a man, love is still worth staying in the game with your arms wide open ready to receive love.

I will give you the tools you need to help keep you from constantly sabotaging your relationships. You will be able to use what you know and make good choices as you enter the dating scene. As Oprah Winfrey often says, "When you know better, you do better!" So, let's learn how to attract better men into our lives!

Steps to Getting over a Broken Heart

If you want to find your perfect partner, you will have to make room for him in your heart. Two things cannot occupy the same space at the same time. If you are still resenting, hurting, or wanting your ex back, there is no room in your heart for Mr. Right. You must clear Mr. Wrong from your heart and mind so that you can receive the love for which you yearn.

So many women are stuck in purgatory because they cannot seem to get over their exes. Later, I will share how I waited on my college sweetheart for more than 13 years and was unable to completely give my heart to a great guy because it was still with my ex – somewhere it was unwanted. DIVAs, please learn from my experience and do not end up wasting your time with a man who is just not feeling you! A man either wants you and sees you as his wife or he doesn't. No amount of begging, pleading, manipulating, wishing, or hoping will change his mind. So, when you are tempted to fight for his love and hold onto him for dear life, breathe, let go, and move on to someone who will admire you and appreciate you for the beautiful queen that you are!

Please note the following suggestions also apply to allowing an ex back into your life if you so choose that path, which I strongly discourage. Here are some steps you can take to break free of heartbreak.

Step #1: Let go

Some of you have dreams regarding your old beau that may have come straight out of the movies. The man, who was a jerk and left you, suddenly realizes that he cannot breathe without you and cannot stand to experience another day without you. He then comes knocking on your door with a rose in his hand

and tears in his eyes, confessing his undying love for you and murmuring, "You complete me." You two then live happily ever after.

Wake up, sister! It's not going to happen. Nine times out of ten, it's over with him. You read correctly. I said that relationship is over, kaput, sayonara, hasta la vista. That ship has sailed, caught fire, and sunk. Let him go! He was the blind jerk who did not have enough common sense to recognize the sexy DIVA who stood right before him. Even if he does come back, he will most likely be the same little shit who broke your heart in the first place. Save yourself the trouble and time and look toward brighter horizons. Even if you insist on getting him back, proceeding as if you are moving on with your life will make you irresistible to your ex.

I've touched on the subject of breaking up so often that I feel like a broken record every time I receive a new email from a heartbroken DIVA or Boo who can't seem to let go of the good memories of their ex. Having one's heart broken not only affects us during the break up, but also impacts us for a long time after the relationship has ended. When you have gotten used to having someone in your life, whether things were good or bad, it can feel like hell facing your life without them. Even when you know deep down that you're better off without him, you still crave contact with him and miss him in a way that can only be compared to an addiction. Deep down you know it's wrong, but you can't seem to help yourself. The cause of your inability to shake this person is most likely due to a soul tie you have with them. A soul tie is a spiritual connection or bondage to someone you've had sex with. I explain soul ties further in Chapter 15 when I discuss sex education for a DIVA.

The truth is that you really do have an addiction, and you must go through the withdrawal in order to feel like a normal person again. Many people return to their destructive relationships because the withdrawal symptoms are so uncomfortable that they just turn around and go back to a mess that should have never been there in the first place. The relationship is over for a reason, and those reasons will not disappear just because you desperately miss your ex. Understandably, your broken heart may have that sinking feeling right now that feels like hunger and fear all mixed up in one and multiplied by 1,000, but it is important that you keep moving forward! Take each day one at a time and put one foot in front of the other. Pretty soon you will start to feel like you have your old self back.

You may feel like it's love, but actually, you are physiologically addicted to the high the relationship causes as your serotonin increases each time you see or think about the ex. Serotonin is a feel-good hormone released in high quantities when people fall in love. Some say that it is this hormone, not love, which causes us to make decisions irrationally early in the relationship.

Your 'addiction' will last as long as you choose to allow it to control your thoughts, feelings, and emotions. This is why, as with any addiction, you must stop cold turkey and leave that jerk who broke your heart alone. Be truthful, the relationship really was not 'all that' to begin with, and you probably should have left a long time ago. You may even remember some of the red flags you encountered along the way. He didn't deserve you and is surely not worth your river of tears.

If the breakup occurred because of your own wrongdoings, forgive yourself and count it as a lesson learned. It may hurt even more knowing that it was your actions or inactions that caused you to lose such a great catch, but do not let this heartbreak occur in vain. Look at yourself in the mirror, be honest with yourself, and make the necessary changes. If it is meant to be, the ex who you lost will forgive you and give you another chance.

I wrote that last paragraph with a bit of hesitancy because I know many of you will make excuses for the ex who walked out of your life and convinced you it was all your fault. If he made you cry more than you laughed and treated you less than you know you deserved, then it was NOT your fault the relationship ended. Be thankful for the great person who is on his way into your life now that you are making room for him.

Although you have been hurt, do not allow your ex to continue to affect you long after the death of your relationship by you choosing to close your heart to new potential love experiences. Let go, move on, and learn better so that the next relationship is the love experience you deserve!

Step #2: Cry

When you realize the relationship is over, take time to mourn your loss. Give yourself permission to cry but with a deadline to cry no more. The loss you mourn will probably be the imaginary relationship you hoped to have. You had hopes and dreams for this relationship and now it's gone. You had what seemed like a chemical addiction, which was just as strong as being addicted to smoking, alcohol, or drugs. It was an addiction to the joy that you thought this man brought or could bring into your life, even if that joy was based on an illusionary relationship that was not 'all that' to begin with. Things always appear better than they actually were when you rationalize them repeatedly.

Here is an activity to try:

Writing Exercise

- Write down all the things that were wrong with your ex on a blank piece of paper.

- On the other side of the paper, write down all the things that were right about him, including the great things he did for you. If the good traits were only present during the first three to six months of your relationship, then they don't count. The first three to six months of a relationship is known as the blissfully fake honeymoon period. Both men and women tend show their flaws after the six-month mark. By then, the real him and you usually appear, and the warm fuzzy feelings float right out the door.

- Once you have finished the list, count the number of good things and the number of bad. If you find yourself stopping to really think about his good traits and what he added to your life, that's because there were not enough of them. Remember the number of good traits you wrote down.

- Now take that piece of paper and tear it up or burn it (Be safe, please).

- Multiply the number of good traits by 100 and know that your perfect partner will be that much better than your ex. The bad traits are the reasons you two broke up and should remind you why you are better off without him.

For some, it will take about one month to get over an ex. For others, it could take up to five years. I hope that you don't take that long because you are just wasting precious time over a dime when a million dollars is waiting for you. Remember, you choose how long you will think about him, how long you will hurt for him, and ultimately how long you will hope that he comes back.

Step #3: Do not communicate with him AT ALL for at least 60 days!

This is a big one. For you to really allow your heart to heal, you need to stop stabbing it with a fork. Seeing and communicating with him while you are still longing to be with him only prolongs your moving on to better horizons. Delete his number from your phone or put his ring tone on silent. Now, for all you DIVAs who think you are so smart that you can get away with texting and emailing him, think again! No communication at all means NO communication at all, and this includes Morse code, sign language, mutual friends, and/or family members you got close to during the relationship. If after 60 days you have not gotten over him, then give yourself another 60 days. When or if you decide to allow him back into your life as a friend — something I strongly advise against — do not allow him to woo you back into his life. Do you really want to start at square one and have to get over the heartbreak again? No, you don't! Allowing him back into your life will only bring you more pain and push back the 30 days to finding the man of your dreams. Just brace yourself for the withdrawal symptoms you will experience, and do not answer his calls, emails, texts, Facebook pokes, pages (young people, you will have to google "pager"), Skype messages, messages in a bottle, or Morse code for at least 60 days.

Step #4: Stay away from the places you know you will run into him.

This includes his home, the club where you met, his favorite sports bar, the gym he goes to on his side of town, and his friends and family member's homes too. Do I really need to tell you that it will be as obvious as 1,2,3 if he sees you showing up at the places he frequents? You will look so desperate, and you may even get your feelings hurt if you see he has moved on with another woman. Cut the ties and let him go. Yes, I know he was great at that thing he did with his tongue. I get that he could make you speak a foreign language you never knew you had learned, but for God's sake, cut him loose so you can begin to heal!

Step #5: No breakup sex

First, why are you having sex with him? Didn't I tell you not to communicate with him for 60 days? Oh, so you did go 60 days but ran into him at the grocery store and happened to fall and slip on his penis on aisle 4. Yeah right! Look, allowing him to reduce you to a booty call to service his needs whenever he wants some great vajayjay will do nothing for your self-esteem.

Look into my crystal ball and see your perfect partner walking into a room and straight to you. He strikes up a conversation by asking your name and where you are from. His eyes reflect a man who is smitten with what he sees and a man of true integrity. You give him your number, and he calls you three times more than you call him. He pursues you. He takes you out and shows you that you are a priority to him. He earns your trust. You do a background check on him, and he is everything and more than you requested on your perfect partner list. Over time, he becomes your best friend, and the two of you fall madly in love. Because there is such a strong connection spiritually, mentally, emotionally, and physically (the lovemaking is off the chain!), together you travel to galaxies you never knew existed. You are so thankful to God that you let that loser ex go because if you hadn't, you would not be lying next to the man of your dreams, the man you are now engaged to, the man who just made you orgasm four times in a row! Now wake up and read every word I have written. Let your ex find another place to get his rocks off because you deserve a soulmate, and he is on his way to sweep you off your feet and love you the way you deserve to be loved!

Step #6: Start a new activity and get a life

Need I elaborate further on this suggestion? Ok, some of you are a little slow, so let me explain. When you focus on something else besides your heartbreak, your lonely nights, and why you are a single woman with no man, it will not only improve your self-confidence, but will also create a sense of satisfaction that allows you to become a whole person before The One comes into your life. Men are attracted to women with a life and women who love themselves enough to have hobbies and activities that make them happy.

Step #7: Meditate

They say that praying is when you talk to God, but meditation is when you listen to what God has to say to you. There is power in stilling your mind from the noise within your head and heart. I know that when your heart has that sinking feeling and your brain is on overdrive thinking about your ex, it is hard to sit still and think about nothing, but I need you to try to meditate every day for at least ten minutes. As you practice daily meditation, you will begin to be in much better control of your thoughts and emotions.

Meditation Exercise

- Meditation can be difficult to do for many people, but I suggest that you start by finding a quiet place within you home that is peaceful for you. The closet is ideal for many people.

- Get a realistic fake candle and turn it on so that you can focus on the flame through your closed lids. The candle doesn't have to be scented, but it may help to light a lavender, sage or lemon-scented candle. Lavender relaxes you, sage allows you to get in touch with your intuition, and the lemon scent provides an emotional boost. Please be careful if you decide to use a real candle. You can also diffuse essential oils.

- Sit with your legs crossed, eyes closed, tongue touching the roof of your mouth, your mouth slightly open, hands on your knees. Be comfortable and just breathe in and out. When thoughts come into your mind, let them come in and float right back out. Do not fight against your thoughts or they will come more frequently. It may be easier to make a sound like "om" and then lower the volume over a minute until it is just a sound in your head. Eventually, allow the sound to go away completely and focus on the candle light or black space in front of your eyes and relax. The goal of meditation is to become as relaxed as you can while quieting the voices in your mind. Like a muscle, your ability to still your mind will get easier as you work at it.

๛ Start your meditation after you are completely relaxed by imagining a white light around your heart. Imagine that this ball of light has magical powers to heal a broken heart. Each day imagine it healing your heart from hurt and disappointment. If you harbor bitterness or ill will toward your ex, close your eyes and imagine that he is in front of you. Tell him that you forgive him and send that white light into his heart and release him.

๛ Know that you are in control of your pain. You determine how long you will hurt. You have the power to say at any moment, "Enough is enough; I chose to move on!"

Step #8: Use Neuro-Linguistic Programming (NLP)

NLP is a big word that simply means using conscious methods to affect the subconscious to create a change in behavior that requires minimum effort to produce. With NLP, a woman can get over her ex more quickly by associating negative sensations to the thoughts of the ex. Your addiction to your ex begins in the mind as a result of repeated thoughts and positive feelings about him. If you play a record over and over, it will eventually become the background music of your life. If you scratch this record, it will never play the same again. Using NLP, you will be able to hinder or stop the repetitive thoughts of your ex and, more importantly, the positive feelings you associate with thoughts of your ex.

NLP Exercise

- Think of something that makes you want to vomit.

- Imagine eating vomit and then rubbing vomit all over your face. Do you feel like throwing up yet? Do you feel sick to your stomach? If so, good.

- Now think of your ex and see his face vividly in front of you.

- Think of the vomit and then think of your ex.

- Do this repeatedly.

If the vomit doesn't cause you a feeling of disgust, think of something else that will create a regurgitation reaction. The more disgusting the thought, the better this technique will work. Eventually, instead of feeling good and getting that high when you think of your ex, you will replace that feeling with disgust and nausea.

Step #9: Repeat positive affirmations

Some of you spend way too much time talking about how wrong someone has done you or how heartbroken you are. Whether you know it or not, you are affirming what you don't want. Your words are powerful, and each word that comes out of your mouth is creating your future. The future you want is with a man who will adore you and treat you like the queen you are. From this day forth, stop verbalizing or thinking about what someone has done to you. Instead, affirm your healing and what you want brought into your life today.

Writing Exercise

- Write down ten of your favorite affirmations for healing and say them to get over your ex.

- Repeat them daily, several times a day. To get over my heartbreak, I constantly repeated this mantra:

"Every day in every way, I am getting over (your ex's name)."

𝓌 See the Affirmations section at the end of this book for lots of other suggestions.

Watch your words and look forward to the happy future that is ahead of you.

Step #10: Know that there are plenty of great guys out there.

Your perfect partner is waiting for you and hoping that you will get over that deadbeat who left or hurt you. Some of you won't stop crying over that man you caught sleeping with your best friend. You can't seem to believe that you can ever love again. You can't seem to believe that plenty of good men out there will love you.

People who choose to fall in love, fall in love every day. That man who hurt you was NOT the only man in the world. In fact, he was nowhere near the best of them. Tell yourself the truth and take a step toward a better future. One day you will see that he was a royal jerk.

If you are wondering why you haven't found love yet or why every woman you seem to meet lately has a man and you don't, it is because they believed that they could get a man. They believed that love would eventually show up at their door. A space was available for love to show up, and when he showed up, they were receptive. Your true love is waiting for you, but *when* you will meet him is up to you. The best thing you can do for your love life is to have the courage to believe that your perfect partner is on his way to you, no matter how badly you have been mistreated or how disappointed you have been with the men who have come in and out of your life. Believe in love, and love will not disappoint you.

❥

Step #11: Start dating

Leave this one to me. I will show you how. Some of you will be absolutely opposed to some of the advice I put forth. But know this: If you continue to do what you have always done, you will continue to get what you have always gotten. You cannot change your life with the same mindset. When you feel resistance rising up in you, take a breath and consider trying what I have suggested. That one thing you say you won't do, could be the one thing you need to do in order to get what you want. How bad do you want to be happy? How bad do you want love? Be open, because lightning could strike!

Warning: Don't be surprised if your ex or exes start to show back up in your life once you have moved on and made the decision to get better. It is almost as if the Universe desires to test us to see if we mean it when we make the decision to receive the greatness that is waiting for us.

I have an online Platinum DIVA University program in which I take between 30-50 women and coach them on a weekly basis for five to seven weeks on the journey to attracting the man of their dreams in less than 30 days. Many women who go through the program report that once they start on the correct love path, their exes show up and hamper their progress. My advice is to not get distracted no matter what he says. Actions speak louder than words. Keep in mind that you want long-term happiness and fulfillment, not a short-term fix. Your ex showing up at this time is just a snapshot of what is waiting for you and a sign that you are getting closer to what it is that you want. If he is really serious about you, he will compete against the other men whom you date.

Do not easily let your ex back in your life to wreak havoc and set you back. You deserve better than that. Set some goals and create your vision board (Chapter 4). Put it in a place where you will see it every day to help keep you focused on what you want to attract into your life.

❤

Chapter 2.
Get Ready to Receive

For those of you with children, from here on out, you will no longer define yourself as a single mother when you are interacting in the dating world. You are a single woman with blessings in the form of children. The term 'single mother' has a historically negative connotation. In the past, when a man left a woman with children, she was considered undesirable or damaged goods.

Although many single fathers can date and find a wife within a relatively short period, the same has not held true for single women. Of course, the tide is turning, and many single women every day are getting married to the man of their dreams. We can easily turn to Hollywood for examples such as Ciara, Charlize Theron, Taraji P. Henson, Vanessa Williams, Demi Moore, Diana Ross, and many others. It will be the same for you. If you think that being a single mother is like wearing a scarlet letter on your forehead, then guess what, the rest of the world will feel the same about you too. If you date and interact with men like the cool DIVA you are, then they will not dwell on the fact that you have a child or children. Your man will grow to accept and love your children as he grows to love you.

Prepare Your Mind

You are tired of sitting home alone on Friday and Saturday nights watching reruns of *Grey's Anatomy*. You are sick of your girls who have stable relationships telling you that the right one will come along soon enough. When you do go out, you are sick of being with your other single girlfriends. Moreover, you are sick of watching loving couples together at the park, movies and restaurants...ugh!

You are probably an intelligent, career-minded woman who has it going on in every area of your life – except the man part, that is. You might believe the myth that the women in your city outnumber men 50 million to 1, and that you are doing great if you catch one with a job, a car, all his teeth, and maybe a nice size south of his navel. Well this myth is CRAP! Throw it out with that jerk who recently broke your heart and know that plenty of GOOD men are out there. Many of these good men are looking for someone as fabulous as you! So, let's get out there and help these poor guys. There are so many men out there that it is realistic to believe you can date three great men a week, if you so wish.

Think of securing your future perfect partner in a similar way to an athlete training for the Olympics. The athlete will set their goal: "Make it to the Olympics." They will prepare themselves physically and mentally. Next, they learn all the rules of the sport and they practice, hard. Finally, they execute the win and achieve their goal of earning an Olympic gold medal. Similarly, you must first set your goal: "Find a wonderful man who will adore you." Next, you need to get fit – physically and mentally – and learn the rules of the dating game and what makes a man tick. Then you practice by dating like a rock star, so you can increase your options. Finally, the time comes to execute and attract the man of your dreams!

Vulnerability is Okay

Two of the most powerful traits that any woman can have are vulnerability and femininity. Vulnerability is the ability to let your guard down enough to let someone in your heart, mind, and space to discover who you truly are. Many women remain single because they have either been 'too available' from a place of insecurity and unworthiness, or they have never learned how to be vulnerable to a man, let alone another person. Many single women have experienced so much disappointment that they have created a wall so thick or high that if their soul mate walked into their life, he would eventually walk out frustrated with trying to get through the wall. Being vulnerable means taking risks. It is easy and safe to keep a boat ashore, but a boat was created to explore the open sea. You were created to love, and to love involves taking a risk. The goal here is to minimize the risk by keeping your eyes open, doing your due diligence, and learning how to attract better quality men into your life!

If you struggle with being vulnerable, you need to practice by working with a DIVA Love Buddy with whom you will share intimate details about your life by answering the journal questions. This will work best if your DIVA Love Buddy is someone you don't really know very well, who you probably met through DIVA University or your DIVA-in-Training group. Another method for increasing vulnerability is to practice asking a stranger for a piece of gum, a dollar, or something small like a cup of sugar. Some of you cringed when I suggested the last sentence because you have gotten so used to making it happen for yourself that you forgot the number one need of almost every man: to be needed. Every man needs to be the top man in your life. He needs to feel as if he can make your life better, but if you cannot allow him to give to you, you will retard the growth process of his love for you.

Enhance Your Femininity

I have said this time and time again: There is power in a woman's femininity. Many women believe that the stereotypical Hollywood-version pretty girls get all the men, but this could not be further from the truth. Straight men are attracted to feminine women. It is a woman's femininity that makes her beautiful and more attractive to the opposite sex. Acting like one of the guys or putting up a tough exterior is not a turn-on for men. A woman does not have to sacrifice her physical appeal because she is a mother by downplaying her femininity and dressing in frumpy, matronly attire.

To clarify, enhancing your femininity has nothing to do with wearing skimpy clothes or applying lots of makeup. Femininity starts on the inside and radiates outward. It is the softness about a woman that demonstrates that she is in touch with her feminine side. Feminine women come in all shapes and sizes and are usually in a relationship or married because men identify them as being excellent mothers and wives.

To enhance your feminine energy, do the feminine/masculine balancing meditation in my meditation audio. Wear feminine colors such as pink and try to avoid dark colors for a while. Here is an exercise that really helps to increase a woman's feminine energy:

Femininity Enhancement Exercise

- While alone in your bedroom, listen to soft music with no clothes on and just move any way that your body is inspired to move.

- Don't do hard dances, just soft, fluid, spontaneous moves.

An energy will rise up within you when you start to do this dance on a daily basis, and if you are a bit on the masculine side, you will start to receive more compliments on your beauty and radiance, as men notice something different about you.

Learn to Receive

Women are nurturing by nature, so once a man does something nice for them, they want to turn around and take over in the giving department to the point where they turn a man off. Especially during the courting phase, a woman must learn how to receive and appreciate a man's sincere overtures.

A man must have an opportunity to give. This is biologically important. In ancient times, men hunted for meat and women gathered other foods and cared for the children. Hunting was dangerous and required special skills – imagine facing down an angry mammoth with nothing but a wood spear with a stone point – and this would have given the man a few thrills along the way. But hunting was important because bringing home the major source of protein was vital to the survival of a man's mate and children.

Echoes of this urge can still be seen in a modern man's body chemistry. When a man starts to fall for a woman, his serotonin increases and testosterone release decreases. This testosterone drop causes a man to exhibit more nurturing qualities such as giving. The instinct to provide is programmed in a man's DNA, and although granted, sometimes that urge is buried pretty deep, a good man will have that instinct, and he will want to give to you. He may want to give you food – think a nice dinner or BBQ on his patio. He may want to give you the gift of an experience such as an evening of dancing or an afternoon of rock-climbing. His gifts may be simple like a bouquet of wild-flowers or repairing of the kitchen sink. But however he expresses his need to give, you must understand it is an important part of his bonding and falling-in-love process. If a woman does not allow a man to give to her, she interrupts this process, and risks losing him.

The other aspect of this ancient hunter programming is that when a woman starts to chase a man, she not only interrupts the biochemical process that makes him want to give to her, she also contradicts the part of him that is a hunter. You will never see a deer walk up to the hunter and say, "Shoot me." The thrill of the hunt is in the fact that the hunter may not catch the deer. Not even a hunter wants the chase to be too easy.

So, ladies, relax. Prepare your mind to receive love, embrace your femininity, let the man come to you, and welcome his gifts joyfully, secure in the understanding that you are a DIVA and deserve all of it! Remember, this courtship is getting you one step closer to snaring that mighty hunter.

Chapter 3.
The Perfect Partner for You

Your perfect partner is the divinely selected partner for you. However, he is not perfect by any means, so get that fantasy out of you head. There is and will never be a perfect man, but there is a perfect man for you. This is why you are reading this book.

What Does a Good Man Look Like to You?

What kind of man do you want? God already knows what you want, as well as what you need, and what the best type of man is for you. In order to move this man from an idea to reality, you must realize what you are looking for, so you can recognize him when he appears. You begin this realization by writing it down. You have to get very specific because if you ask for "a man", you will get what you have asked for: a man. However, will he be all that you want and need in a man? You would never go house hunting for a home without having a good idea of the features you desired in the home – would you? Do you even know what a good man looks like? What does it feel like for this kind of man to love you? To help you get a good grasp on what sort of man you want, I suggest a series of exercises.

Writing Exercise

- Write down what a good man looks like.

- Write what if feels like for a good man to love you.

It is important to understand that a relationship is like the legs of a chair; if one leg is missing, the chair will not stand. You must be emotionally, physically, mentally, and spiritually compatible with your perfect mate. Keep this in mind when you are deciding what type of man may be your perfect partner.

What Does Your Future Perfect Partner and Best Friend Look Like?

Now you'll make a list to describe your perfect partner's qualities. Putting it in writing is like using a catalog to construct the man of your dreams. Using the activity that follows, make a list of qualities that you desire in your future soulmate.

Writing Exercise

ℓ Make a list of the qualities you desire in your future perfect partner and best friend.

What Are Your Non-Negotiables?

Think about the characteristics that you absolutely cannot tolerate or cannot live without. When you make this list, it is very important to keep your statements in the affirmative. For example, my original list stated that my ideal man must not smoke, drink too much, or be abusive. I changed the line item to state: "Must value his body and treats it like a temple." A person who treats their body like a temple will not use drugs, over-eat, or drink too much, but I put the intention in the affirmative so that the focus is on what I *do* want – not on what I *do not* want.

Writing Exercise

ℓ Make a list of six non-negotiable characteristics of your perfect partner.

Most of us walk around saying that we "don't want" a man to be a cheater, liar, or to mistreat us; and then when he shows up in our life as a cheating, lying abuser, we are surprised. Well, this is because you will attract what you focus on even if you don't want it. This is called the Law of Attraction. We live in a Universe with laws that are just as solid as the law of gravity. What goes up, must come down. Whatever belief you repeat over and over to yourself will become true, even if the belief is false and does not serve you. Words plus thoughts plus emotion are the ingredients of manifesting. If you have been wondering why you have been praying to God for a good man but remain single, it is because you prayed, doubting he will come. Each time you pray with fear or doubt, you are drawing to you that which you fear. You screamed with strong emotion that, "All men are dogs!" when your ex cheated on you or disappointed you. That energy you felt at the time lodged itself in your cells, and that belief sunk into your subconscious mind where it has been working behind the scenes to create your (negative) experiences even when you are not trying.

To undo this, you must use the Law of Attraction to work in your favor by repeating the affirmations in the back of the book with feeling. Pray with absolute faith. Anytime you say something negative and do not want to deal with the consequences of what you will attract with those words, repeat "cancel, cancel, reset." Spend time writing notes to yourself describing the future you will have with your future husband. Finally, visualize yourself being loved long-term. You must feel the emotion throughout your body that love will show up. The Law of Attraction states that you will attract anything you focus upon for a long enough period of time or with enough feeling.

So, start using your mind to bring what you do want, which is a good man who adores you, respects you, and treats you like the queen you are!

What Are the Characteristics of Your Perfect Partner?

Now think back to all your exes. For some of you, that list is very long, or you can't remember that far back, so pick the ones you really liked or even loved. What about him did you love so much? What gave him the 'it' factor?

Let me explain the 'it' factor for all of you who are wondering why this is on my list. Think back to a time when you and your girlfriends were just hanging out together or standing around at work when a man approached who made you all do a double take. Although he was confident, he was not arrogant, and his humility was charming. You could tell by looking at him that he was a man's man, not a pushover you could easily dominate. Although, none of you knew this man personally, you knew that something was drawing you to him like a magnet. This kind of man will keep your attention and keep you interested, but it is important that you attract the 'Good Guy' type and not the 'Bad Boy'. This characteristic is important when looking for a long-term mate because when most people settle down, they get comfortable and very bored with the relationship. The man with the 'it' factor will keep you on your toes, and that's what you want. Trust me on this one!

Now, do a meditation in which you call God into your heart.

Meditation Exercise

- ❧ Take five deep breaths and envision a ball of green light surrounding your heart.

- ❧ Visualize this green light growing to fill your entire body. Thank God for the person that has been set aside for you.

- ❧ Ask for God's will to bring the right person for you.

- ❧ Ask God to allow you to see your soul mate and reveal what characteristics in him will make you happy.

♥

You may or may not see or hear anything, but you will be more aligned with God's intentions for you after doing this meditation. You are now ready to do the following exercise.

Writing Exercise

- Write down the characteristics you saw in your Perfect partner during your meditation. Let your heart, not your mind, take over and do the writing.

- Is he ambitious, professional, honest, or an animal lover? (If he loves animals, he is sensitive to human emotions. This is a good one!)

- Is he fun to be around, dependable (does what he says he will do when he says he will do it)?

- Is he close to his mom but not a Mama's Boy?

- Does he like nature? I think you get the picture here. The idea is to get very detailed because you are sculpting a masterpiece.

- Place a star next to ten characteristics that you must have in your man. You will have to compromise on some characteristics because, as I stated before, no perfect man exists anywhere on Earth. You know yourself better than anyone else and what personality traits you must have in your man to be happy with him for the rest of your life.

What Does your Perfect Partner Look Like?

I can already hear your minds going a million miles an hour on this one. Yes, his appearance is an important factor. It's not an absolute factor but at least write down your desired features in your future mate. I am not saying that he has to be attractive to the world, but he must be attractive to you. For all of you who are a bit inflexible, this section is somewhat more flexible than the other sections. You can deviate if he is hitting all of your other wish-list items. Just make sure he is someone attractive enough to turn you on. You must be able to kiss him with the lights on! His personality alone will not satisfy you sexually.

Just imagine the best features of the men you have dated, loved in the past, seen on TV, seen on the street, admired at work or wherever, and write them down. Is he tall, short, bald, pretty eyes, nice smile, a big butt, not too thin or overweight? You may like thick guys or 'teddy bears', as I call them. If so, write that down! Does he have nice teeth or honest eyes? Oh, yes, he must have the "it" factor in the physical department too!

Writing Exercise

- Write down the physical features you desire in your perfect partner.

What Kind of Spirituality Does Your Perfect Partner Have?

Even if you are not the most religious person, selecting someone that you are spiritually compatible with is important. Does he share the same spiritual beliefs and religion as you do? Does he even believe in a higher power? Does he pray? Does he go to church? Is he active in the church? Is he open to praying or worshiping with you even if you both do not share the same religion? Just make sure that you have a good idea of how spiritually compatible and connected you two are. I am a huge believer that if you believe in a Higher Power and have a relationship with God, then your perfect partner MUST also be a man who has submitted to this Higher Power. Relationships go through enough challenges without having to fight about spiritual beliefs.

Writing Exercise

- Write down the spiritual attributes you want in your Perfect partner.

What Kind of Relationship Do You Want?

Think of your favorite loving couple. What do they look like when they are together? Now think of similar experiences you want with your perfect partner. Do you bring out the best in each other? Are you best friends? Can you share your secrets with him? How often do you have sex? Do people envy your love? Do you solve disagreements easily? Are you faithful to each other?

If you have experienced destructive relationships all your life, know that it does not have to be that way forever. Your past does not dictate your future any more than the fact that it rained yesterday means it will rain today. Look at the mistakes you have made in your relationships and what was missing and write down what you want to experience from here on out.

Writing Exercise

- Write down what elements in a relationship are important to you.

- What will your relationship with your perfect partner be like?

In the exercises in this chapter, you have imagined every detail of your perfect partner and written it all down. You are activating the Law of Attraction by focusing on all the wonderful things that you do want, instead of those things you never want again. Your perfect partner is now on his way to you. The next step is preparing yourself so that you are ready for him when he arrives.

Chapter 4.
Preparing Yourself

Now that you have an image of the perfect mate for you written down on paper, commit every night to focusing on bringing him into your life. Doing visualizations is a powerful way to begin to experience the feelings associated with having what you desire in your life.

Begin with Mental Work

If you have received nothing from me yet, please receive that your progress and attainment of any goal, especially attracting a good man, starts in the mind first. If I can get you thinking right, then everything else can fall into place. Every day, I want you to wake up with a grateful heart for all your blessings. In your mind say, "Thank you God for my family, my mind, health, my body, my home, etc.", and feel the sense of thanksgiving growing within your heart and moving throughout your body. The more powerful the feeling, the stronger the attraction. Refrain from complaining at least until noon.

In addition, do the Perfect Partner Meditation, below, at least 5 times a week. It is extremely powerful for attracting your soulmate. If you are able to get my meditation CD, it includes this Perfect Partner Meditation along with other meditations. Enough with the shameless plug; let's get started!

Meditation Exercise

- Lie comfortably in your bed and play the sound of the ocean, rain, or a waterfall.

෧ Close your eyes and imagine yourself walking on a beautiful beach. Feel the sand under your feet. Hear the ocean all around you. Smell the salt water in the air.

෧ Now, stand still and thank God or your higher power for delivering your perfect partner to you. Feel the feeling of gratitude all over your body.

෧ Imagine looking down at your stomach and seeing a ball of white light growing bigger and bigger in your stomach and moving up through your chest, past your heart, up through your throat, into your face, and out the top of your head. See the bright white light float in front of you.

෧ Look in the distance and imagine another bright white light moving toward you and your bright light. This white light moving toward you is your perfect partner.

෧ See the two lights moving closer toward each other until they finally touch and become one.

෧ Hold this image for a while. You may experience a tingling feeling as if you are floating in the air.

෧ See your soulmate materialize out of his bright white light and see yourself materialize out of your white light. Visualize the way he looks, the way it feels to be held in his arms, and the way he looks deep into your eyes with so much love, acceptance, and respect. You should know that he has most, if not all the traits you desire in your future love. Feel the love you share for each other. Imagine the love you both have for your children (if that's what you want or currently have), and then feel this love for him.

෧ Know that when you release him back into the Universe, he will return to you when the time is right.

෧ Now imagine him transforming back into the ball of white light, and with your hands around the white ball, release him. See him float away into the heavens and know silently that you will see him again in your meditation tomorrow.

🍃 Do this meditation every night before you go to sleep. This exercise is so powerful that you start to feel as if the love you will feel when you finally find The One is here now.

Develop DIVA Confidence

From this day forward, you are a DIVA (Divine, Intelligent, Vivacious, and Alluring). I will go further into why a DIVA is a woman who significantly increases her chances of finding a good man later in this book, but for now, remember that as a DIVA you are:

Divine

Every woman is a divine creation of God and should value herself and body as such.

Intelligent

Intelligence is attractive, and no woman should dumb herself down to attract or keep a man.

Vivacious

This means "having vitality and life." Nothing is more beautiful than a woman who loves life, walks with a bounce in her step and consistently sees the bright side of living.

Alluring

You are a queen, a man magnet. Your confident demeanor, class and self-value lures men to you. You do not have to chase any man – ever! You do not have to have sex with just anyone who wants it. No one wants anything if it is too easy. A true DIVA does not give her heart, mind, or body to any man unless he first earns it. She sits back, knowing her worth and value and draws love to her.

A DIVA is not born; she is created. You must train your mind to become a DIVA Whenever you walk into a room full of people, repeat to yourself, "I am a man magnet, and every man in this room wants to know who I am!" This will cause your stroll to change into a stride and your look to radiate, saying, "I have a secret you need to know, and the secret is that I am the most amazing woman this side of the Mississippi River!" This attitude is how you develop the 'it' factor. If you tell yourself enough positive things, you will eventually believe them; and this, my friends, is what separates the women from the DIVAs.

Everything about a DIVA radiates confidence. To have confidence means to look your flaws in the face while focusing on your strengths and carrying yourself with an air that radiates that you love yourself unconditionally. The difference between a frustrated single woman and a DIVA is that a DIVA has confidence, and because of this, she is very appealing to the opposite sex.

I heard a story about a woman with muscular dystrophy who was a paraplegic when she met her husband, but still carried herself with confidence. Although she has been confined to a wheelchair for most of her life, she is a radiant woman who was able to attract a good man who is not disabled and who loves and cares for her daily. They have been married for more than 20 years.

Confidence is the most attractive perfume you can wear, and with it, you will attract men like you have never imagined. If you have a hard time moving past your insecurities and walking with confidence, I suggest that you keep doing your affirmations with feeling. You may want to turbo boost your results by repeating the affirmation for the week throughout the day non-stop every time you think about it.

Heal Your Issues

Every woman wants to be able to find her knight in shining armor, fall madly in love, and live happily ever after. I cannot say this enough: Finding a man is the easy part, but who exactly are you finding? Do you want *a* man, or do you want the *right* man? In order to be ready to attract the man of your dreams, you must first be whole emotionally, mentally, and spiritually. If you are single and have had a string of bad relationships, you likely have a limiting belief that is holding you back from love. I will show you how to heal these issues and free your heart to attract and receive a healthy love experience.

Let your past pain go. You cannot put new wine into old wine skins. You cannot be open to a good man unless you first let go of your ex-man. Forgiveness is the name of the game, and it is a must for you to forgive any man, including your father, for the pain he may have caused.

Do the Burning Ritual

This is a very powerful ritual for transforming your pain into a gift that will give you the ability to love at a level that is deeper than anything that you have ever experienced.

Writing Exercise

- Take a piece of paper and write a letter to the person who injured you. Address the letter:

  "Dear _____ (name or names of the person/people who hurt you),
  I just want to share with you how much you really hurt me."

- Next, write specifically what they did to hurt you. In my case, I wrote:

  "Daddy, I loved you so much, and I never felt like I was able to earn your love. The things that you said to me growing up were so painful that I still reflect and cry about them to this day. I do not have words to describe how much it hurt to have you not show up at my wedding. I do not believe that there is any excuse to not be there on one of your

daughter's most significant days. Every time I try to believe that you changed, you hurt me again."

~ After you write what the person did to hurt you, express how his or her actions made you feel and what effect it has had on your life. I wrote:

"Every time you did not show up for me as the hero whom I grew up thinking that you were, I felt lost and unprotected. This feeling of vulnerability pushed me to create a shell around myself that prevented anyone from really ever getting too close to me. This left me feeling empty, as if I was missing some life experience God had for me."

~ Finally, tell the person that you forgive him or her, and ask the person to forgive you as well for any hurt that you may have unknowingly caused. If you were raped, violated, or hurt by a person in which you have no attachment or further contact, forgive on behalf of the person who hurt your offender. Ask your offender to forgive the person(s) who hurt him/her so badly that he/she was able to inflict his/her hurt upon you in that way. I wrote:

"Daddy, I want you to know that I forgive you and ask that you forgive me too for judging you and for anything that I have done unknowingly to hurt you. I recognize that you must have felt extreme pain to be unable to love me in a manner in which a father should love his child. I wish nothing but great things to happen for you, and I ask God that you be blessed."

~ Yes, you are going to ask for the well-wishes or blessing of the person who hurt you. This is the most important step in healing and letting go of the pain that is crippling you. You cannot hate someone and receive love at the same time. Your hate, resentment, and unforgiveness is preventing you from receiving the love that you deserve to have in your life.

- You will write this letter but NEVER SEND IT! That's right. Never mail or give this letter to the person you are writing it about. This letter is for you and your healing.

- Take this letter and place it under a white seven-day jar candle. Burn this candle in a safe location for seven days with the letter under the candle and ask for God to heal your hurt, forgive this person, and bless the individual in all he or she does.

For many of you, this will be a very difficult task to do. This is why I am sharing my story with you. It was not easy to forgive my dad, ask for God to bless him, and to really let go of what I believed he did to me. However, I thought of it this way: I could go on hating him while killing myself, my life, and my future, as I eliminated all opportunities for a happy love experience; or I could let it go, heal, and receive a healthy love experience beyond my wildest imagination. Holding on to the resentment, hate, and negative feelings of those who hurt and betrayed you is so not worth it, and I wanted so much more out of life! If you really want this program to work for you, you will have to make the decision to release your past hurts, limiting beliefs, and fears.

- After the seven days of praying for the person who injured you to be forgiven and blessed and for your own healing and blessing, go to a safe place and burn the letter. (Please do not set the house on fire and blame me. I take no liability for any burnt fingers that occurred as a result of this activity, so be careful!)

- Do not do the burning part of the ritual yet if your heart has not yet started to feel lighter and you still have not yet begun to forgive your offender. Give yourself another week if necessary or seek a professional if the pain is unbearable for you and you are unable to get over it alone.

Remember, there is nothing wrong with seeking professional help. After my divorce, I hurt so bad and had such a hard time forgiving my ex for cheating on me that I hated men with a passion and it was difficult for me to believe that I could ever meet someone who would not betray me in some way. I had such a hard time moving past all my limiting beliefs about men that I paid well over $10,000 to work with a life coach until I was able to get over it. I did not have $10,000 and I was a single mother at the time, but I knew that I had to make it happen if I wanted better for myself and my kids, so I opened a credit card and made it happen. Counseling and coaching have been the bedrock of my ongoing healing and my ability to finally attract love. I recommend that if you need coaching, get the assistance you need along with using this book to attract the man of your dreams.

Get coaching

(*Warning: Shameless plug ahead.*) Not all coaches are created equal. Find the right coach whom you trust can help you and follow every detail of their coaching. I have a 98% success rate as a certified dating and relationship coach. There are a lot of life coaches out there but not many certified dating and relationship coaches trained in hypnotherapy, neuro linguistic programing, and subconscious healing. I am gifted at 'reading' my clients' past, present, and future life paths and identifying the problem with the help of spiritual guidance. I can also do remote healings (heal across distances). No, I do not use witchcraft or evil methods. According to the Christian Bible, my abilities are nothing new and are promised to every human being who accepts Jesus' promise of being able to "do greater than He." I have had this gift since I was a child and refined it with training by studying with spiritual masters. If you are unfamiliar with any of this, please do not dismiss it as hocus pocus or think I am crazy. Keep an open mind and keep reading. In addition, I have been coaching for a long time and am good at what I do because I have studied the science of human behavior and what works to create change. I have a high success rate with helping my clients not only attract love but to ultimately get married. As a result, there is an investment in working with me – but all my clients can confirm that it's worth it.

As I have increased my coaching prices, my success rate has also increased. I used to provide coaching at a low cost and sometimes gave advice for free but quickly discovered that this did not benefit me or my clients. Almost all the clients who have received my advice for free, never follow the advice I gave them. Most whom I charged very little to work with me, had a low success rate. My high success rate clients always invest in themselves by doing what it takes to get coaching. There is something powerful about having skin in the game.

After attending a Tony Robbins conference, I decided to start charging more for my coaching. I'd been successfully coaching for six years and had many success testimonials but was disappointed with the rate of clients who were unable to attract love. I was afraid of charging too much and losing out on attracting clients. Tony Robbins helped me discover that the right clients, who value my services, will gladly pay for my help and most likely will follow my coaching advice much better. I was already in the middle of coaching a client who'd only paid me $1500 for my six weeks coaching package. She was very difficult to work with and often challenged me on my advice. After her six weeks, I decided not to continue working with her. She is still single today. On the other hand, my first client after that conference, who gladly paid me $4500 for a six weeks telephone coaching package, followed every step of my advice and attracted her husband a month after working with me. The cost was a stretch for my client, but she made it happen. The sacrifice fueled her to complete her homework, follow my advice, and do the work to attracting her soul mate. She later told me that I was under-charging and that the love she experiences daily with her husband is worth much more than the $4500 she paid and that she would have gladly paid triple. This was confirmation to decrease the number of private clients I accept and raise my prices. I have been on a roll ever since!

I tell you this this to say, don't look for the cheapest coach or the most convincing. There are a lot of 'experts' out there. Check out their testimonials, listen with your heart to their advice, interviews, and videos. Ask your spirit if this is the person whom you should work with and follow that guidance. Once you select a coach, especially if the price is high, make it happen and do the work to make that coaching relationship work for you.

Repeat daily affirmations

Like I said earlier, the Law of Attraction is at work whether you are making it work in your favor or not. The use of affirmations makes it work for you.

Affirmation Exercise

- ⟋ I have included a suggested affirmation list in the back of this book. Each week of the 30 days includes a different affirmation for attracting what you want.

- ⟋ Say the affirmations twice daily: first thing in the morning and right before going to bed. Make sure that you are looking into the mirror while repeating these affirmations, feeling the strong emotions grow throughout your body as you repeat them.

- ⟋ Repeat the affirmation the number of times of your age. For example, if you are 26 years old, repeat the affirmation for that week 26 times while looking in the mirror in the morning and again at night. Affirmations only work if you repeat them with strong emotion over and over throughout the day.

Cancel negative words and thoughts.

Whenever I work with women helping them attract love, I always find a way to identify their limiting beliefs and the negative language or thoughts that are standing in their way.

Think about the negative thoughts or things that you have repeated to your friends or anyone else that contradict what you want. For instance, some women truly believe that all men cheat, all men are dogs, and all men lie. Other women fear that all relationships end in divorce and cannot even imagine themselves being married, let alone in a healthy relationship. These thoughts are barriers that must be overcome in order to attract a good man into your life.

Whenever you speak, you are praying and invoking the Law of Attraction. When you say something negative, you have 16 seconds to 'delete' its creation of future consequences. The best way to erase the effects of a limiting thought is to say "cancel, cancel, reset" out loud or in your mind when you find yourself repeating out loud or internally one of your negative beliefs. Be consistent and repeat it even if you are around your friends or other people. You do not want to leave your limiting beliefs in the mind of someone else because they will repeat that belief back to you, which will work negatively toward attracting what you want. From this day forward, not a negative word, thought, or belief will cross your mind or lips unchecked.

Writing and Affirmation Exercise

- Make a list of the negative thoughts you tend to repeat.

- Go through the list, and for each one read it out loud, followed by the words, "Cancel, cancel, reset!"

- Then, burn the list in a safe manner and release those negative thoughts into the wind.

Look in the mirror

Look in the mirror. What is your first reaction? Do you like what you see? Can you say, "I love you, girl," and mean it without wanting to run out of the room? I get emails every day from women who hate their looks and for whatever reason believe that they are undesirable to men. They hate their weight, their appearance, their height, etc., and wonder why they can't seem to find someone who will want or love them. Look, DIVA, if you do not love you and accept you where you are, no one else will. You are the only YOU you will ever have, so get used to it! Nothing is more unattractive than a woman with low self-esteem having a daily pity party. Love you, and you will attract a man who will love you too!

Become what you want

Did you write down characteristics on your wish list for your perfect partner that you do not yet possess? You cannot ask for a characteristic you are unwilling to possess. If you want him to be an honest man but you lie like a rug, then you will attract a liar.

Writing Exercise

- Get out the list you wrote of things you want in your perfect partner.

- Draw a heart around the numbers of the characteristics you do not yet possess.

- Now, get to work on possessing these traits. Do not rush this process. Sometimes it takes months to be ready for love. It will be worth it in the end if you give yourself time to focus on healing and loving you.

Create Space in Your Life

As I stated before, you cannot have what you want if you have no room to receive. When you act as if you already have something, this creates an irresistible magnetism for drawing that thing into your life. You will see amazing results when you follow my advice and start to create space in your life for your soul mate. Here are some tips:

- Clear some drawer, closet and table space for him.
- Throw away old lingerie you have used with someone else.

- Remove pictures from your wall that show just a single woman or anything that contradicts marriage.
- Add pictures all around you of happy couples or families.
- If you work over 40 hours a week, cut back and make time to date and spend time with the future partner you are getting ready to attract into your life.
- Prepare a table setting for your future husband daily.
- Always have a pair of roses in your home.
- If you burn a candle, always burn two.
- Send positive thoughts and prayers to your future husband.

Plan Your Wedding

I know that this may seem crazy or feel weird, but I suggest that you get a wedding planning book and start to plan your wedding – but only *after* you have worked on and healed your issues. Do not put any money down on anything or book any venues or rental supplies. This is a spiritual rather than a physical activity.

Like an architect, you are planning what will be in the future. Of course, you will be open-minded and flexible, understanding that your future perfect partner may not want the wedding colors that you choose, but this is alright because you understand that it is his wedding too. Do not show anyone your wedding planning book because it is just for you, and you do not want the guy you eventually start dating to think that he is just a warm body to fill the role you have already planned before he came into your life.

Before I met my husband, I was inspired to start planning my wedding. I purchased several wedding magazines, a wedding planning book and cut out pictures of the way I wanted my dream wedding to be. Ultimately, our wedding was nothing like I planned it, but the vibration created from putting myself in the space of planning a wedding made attracting my future husband very real to me.

While planning your wedding, do not say to yourself that you do not want this or do not want that because you are unable to afford it. Just let go and act as if money is no object and dream your fairytale wedding. The point of the exercise is to get you feeling the positive emotions of planning your own wedding. As you start to feel these emotions, getting married will become more of a reality to you that you can come to accept. If you cannot see yourself married, you will never get married. You must see it first before it materializes.

Exercise Your Body

Exercising applies to everyone, whatever size they may be. Exercising is not only good for the body; it is good for the mind. A woman who takes care of her body is not only a healthy woman, but a happy, strong, and confident woman as well. As you will see later in this book, confident women are extremely attractive to men. These women are the type who will love themselves enough not to let anyone walk all over them. Men like strong women who love and care about their appearance, well-being, and health.

Join an Activity

Yes, ladies, please get a life aside from the demanding job of either being a mother and/or your 9-to-5 where you work like a slave. Do something that will be 'your' time and allow you to develop a hobby while meeting new friends. Making your kids or your job your focus is understandable and necessary, but it isn't healthy or beneficial to you or your children if you don't have those other activities just for you. Many single women get burned out and become severely depressed, bitter, and angry, taking out their frustration out on their friends, family, their children, or co-workers. When you have a fulfilling well-rounded life, you will also invite love to find you. In turn, finding love is like food for the soul that not only nourishes you but revitalizes your relationship with the people you care most about. It's a beautiful cycle.

♥

In addition, a single woman who has been out of the dating or social scene for a long time is often unskilled at meeting and interacting with men on a social level. The sad reality for many of these women is that they give up on love and base their entire lives on their work, children, or other relationships only to miss an opportunity for a beautiful love experience. Do yourself, your children, or your dog a favor; GET OUT OF THE HOUSE AND GET A LIFE!

Look Fly at ALL Times

I know that it sounds high maintenance or perhaps undesirable to attempt to look good ALL of the time, but you must at least look good enough to meet your husband for the first time every time you walk out of your door. It is obvious that you will look fly when you are hanging out with the girls or when you are on your way to work, but you are a woman with a plan, and a woman with a plan is a powerful woman indeed! Look great even if you are running to the store, the library, or the soccer game. You just never know when Mr. Right will cross your path, and what a shame it would be if you looked like you just rolled out of bed when he decided to go hunting for you. Men are always looking, so make a habit of always being prepared. Not to mention, dressing as if you could meet your husband at any time will put you in the energy of expectation at all times. This energy is powerful for attracting what you want in life.

Need I go to the Bible and tell you about the maidens who were waiting for the bachelor. (Ok, I am ad-libbing here, but stay with me.) Some of them were prepared and had oil for their lamps and the others were unprepared and ran out of oil while waiting for the bachelor to appear. The unprepared maidens had to run to the store to get some more oil. We all know what happened next. While they were gone, the bachelor appeared, and the prepared maidens got the man! Don't be like the unprepared maidens. Always be prepared!

Have a Big Enough 'Why'

My dear lovely ladies, here is the secret to how well this program will work for you. When I say have a big enough 'why,' what I mean is to determine what drives you to want a relationship. Do you *really* want a relationship, and if so, *why* do you want a relationship? The answer to why has to be powerful or inspirational enough to motivate you to find your soulmate, no matter what. Otherwise, your why is not big enough; it is not enough to fuel and sustain your journey. For example, maybe your answer to 'why?' was, "I'd like to meet someone nice because I don't want to be alone on Christmas." The activity below will guide you on how painful it would feel for you to spend every Christmas for the rest of your life without someone special. If you look over your answers to your why, and if you have not stated something that brings you to tears, then your why is not big enough. Your answers must create so much emotion that you cannot keep the tears from flowing. So, let me show you how to create a big 'why'.

Writing & Visualization Exercise

- Get a piece of paper and write down WHY you want a healthy relationship that will eventually lead to a happy marriage.

- Start by imagining your life 5, 10, and 20 years from now if you never meet your soulmate. Imagine how dull and unhappy your life may be if you never attract the perfect partner to share your life. Understand that this process will get really uncomfortable, but no matter what, you will not quit. The more emotional that you feel, the better, so when negative feelings come over you and you want to start crying, go ahead and cry.

- Keep writing and envisioning your life as a single woman forever. How does it feel to never have a husband to take to the Christmas party? Being single is very expensive and you are missing out on having a partner in the trenches with you building a nest egg to enjoy the future with. It is also stressful knowing that if you were ever to be laid off, who would have your back and handle the bills? What if you ever get sick, lose a parent, break your foot, etc.? These are very real scenarios that should motivate you past your fears of failing. I know that you may be an independent woman who may say to yourself, "If I stay single my whole life, it is just not meant for me to be with anyone, and I will be just fine with me and my Jesus!" Well, we already agreed that if this were the case, you would not be here reading this book, so push that crazy notion out of your mind. Be brave enough to feel the loss of not getting what you really want.

- If you are feeling really down right now, this is good.

- Intensify this feeling. Imagine feeling all the loneliness and stress of spending the rest of your life alone. Imagine no one to lie next to you and hold you through the night. Imagine no sex with someone with whom you feel safe and loved. Imagine being an old lady with lots of cats and birds but no children or memories of a happy life with your soulmate.

- What does it feel like knowing the reason you are alone in this future is not because of any flaw you think that you have but because of the fears you refuse to relinquish? Are your fears worth it? Are they worth pushing love away and continuing to repeat the same negative behaviors, thoughts, beliefs and feelings about love and relationships over and over again in your head? Is your happiness worth it?

- I know this doesn't feel good and that you are feeling pretty terrible right now but intensify this feeling and make it stronger. Scream if you want to as you feel the agony pour throughout your body.

- Now breathe.

- Stand up and shake your body loose.

- Go wash the tears off your face and get another piece of paper.

- Now make a list of what life will look like in 5, 10 and 20 years when you attract your soul mate. Are you excited that your family will share picnics, holidays, and days at the fair together? Imagine the family portraits you will take together. Can you imagine your beautiful wedding day? Imagine yourself on the porch when you grow old holding hands with your soulmate. Do you play together? Make great love together? Can you see your future children with him?

- How do you feel right now as you are making this list? If you do not feel extreme joy, then you need stronger reasons and visions of what your future will look like when you attract your soulmate to you. Fight the temptation to say, "This will never happen for me anyways so why bother." This is just a self-defense mechanism that goes up when you are feeling vulnerable and at risk for disappointment. If you make a 'why' strong enough, you will not have to worry about failing to attract the right person. He will show up if you do everything I am sharing with you and believe that it can and will happen for you.

- Feel a sense of certainty that your husband appearing in your life is as certain as you blinking your eyes, scratching your nose, or falling asleep tonight. When you feel this certainty, intensify the feeling and allow it to take over your body. Start laughing if you want, smile from ear to ear, and jump up and down at the excitement of the future you will have with your soul mate.

Create a Relationship Vision Board

If you attend most success seminars, you will be told to create a vision board. A vision board is simply a compilation of pictures that reflect what you want to manifest in your life. You place the vision board in a place where you will see it every day because it will remind your subconscious mind what you want to attract. It will also keep you focused on your goal, so you don't settle or get sidetracked from the goal.

You create a vision board by finding pictures from sources such as magazines or the Internet and arranging them on a plain white board. In DIVA University, some participants create a vision board as a digital collage on their computers. Some have even made it their screensavers.

A relationship vision board should include a picture(s) representing the happy couple you would like to be, a wedding dress, a man proposing, and a family with children, if you desire kids. I recommend that you include a picture of your home, car, desired career goal, ideal physique, and one representing spiritual growth. Your vision board should include 60 percent pictures reflecting your relationship desires and the rest showing other areas and goals in your life. Envision it all because it is possible to have it all if you so choose.

Creative Exercise

- Create a physical or digital (I prefer physical) vision board focused on the life you want to create with your perfect partner.

- Keep this vision board someplace where you can see it daily and use it to power the Law of Attraction as you bring your dream into reality.

The bottom line is that you must prepare yourself and your life to receive The One and all the love he brings into your life. You do this by developing your confidence, healing your issues, creating space in your life, and dating with tenacity and a purpose. If you are prepared when he shows up, you can avoid a lot of the pitfalls that come with getting ready while being in a relationship.

Chapter 5.
Avoiding The 'Don't Wanters'

Some men are damaged goods, tainted, and simply, for the birds. We DIVAs are looking for the best, drama free, supportive men we can attract. Following your gut instincts to weed out the undesirables is important. God, the Divine, Spirit, intuition, or whatever you choose to call your higher power *always* sends us a warning, a sign, or a feeling in the form of our gut instincts.

We get that feeling that something just isn't right, but then we talk ourselves out of it. We use the excuse that we are being extra picky or overly cautious because we have been hurt in the past. However, when you feel that something isn't right, please do not ask questions, do not pass GO, and do not collect $200. Stop, pay attention, and look for the exit sign if you sense something is wrong. Run as fast as you can in the opposite direction of him. Nothing is worse than wasting your time on a jerk you had a 'feeling' about early in the relationship, but you did not listen and wasted precious time that could have been used finding your perfect partner. We have all met different variations of these guys. STAY AWAY from any of these men.

The Woman Hater

His mother mistreated him, he had his heart broken by a girl in the first grade, or he never got a date to his high school prom. These men, for whatever reason, hate women. The idea of breaking a woman's heart excites them. Men who are Woman Haters are misogynistic, narcissistic, controlling, and abusive. They no longer have the natural human ability to sympathize with another human.

A Woman Hater will slowly strip the strong-minded woman's self-esteem as he mentally, verbally, and even physically abuses her, and leaves her wondering, "How did I get here?"

How can you tell he is a Woman Hater? He will degrade other women at any chance he gets by calling them bitches and hoes. He will talk poorly about his ex, other women he has dated, his friends' girlfriends, and even complain about his mother. If he mistreats his mother, his exes, other women at work, and the dog, it is safe to say he will not treat you any better. This guy is the worse type of guy to date or marry and can possibly set you up for the next available spot in the psych ward or the mortuary. Don't walk, skip, or even run. Sprint the hell away from this crazy, deranged punk who would become your worst nightmare.

What Happened to Me: After Terry, one of my college sweethearts, and I broke up, I was devastated and vulnerable, willing to do anything to get rid of the heartbreak feeling. I hurt so bad that I wanted nothing more than to replace the pain with loving someone else. When I met Kevin two weeks after the breakup, I fell for him the first time I heard him speak. Kevin was extremely popular on campus and held thought-provoking discussions that fed my hunger for knowledge. He also reminded me a lot of my beloved ex. Kevin's birthday was one day before Terry's, and they had a lot of personality traits in common, including being liked and respected by most everyone on campus. Therefore, for the first and last time in my life, I made the dreaded mistake of having sex with a man (Kevin) on the first night. This mistake led to my eyes becoming foggy to the Avoiding the Don't Wanters truth about this man. Although I saw signs early on that he was abusive, I still moved to Georgia with him after my graduation when I was four months pregnant. I know, I know! Yes, I got pregnant within months of dating him.

I miscarried the week after I graduated from college, but I wanted my baby back so bad that I got pregnant a month later in what I would say was one of my most abusive, turbulent relationships ever. We would get into very nasty arguments in which he would call me all kinds of names, grab me, push me, and even punch me in the face. One day, I guess I got fed up with the abuse because, that day, I did a Tina Turner on him and whooped his a@*. It was about 3 a.m. and we got into an argument about the covers. I must have said something that he didn't like because all I remember was that he came charging at me in the dark while I sat in the bed, and I punched him in the face to defend myself. What happened after that was beyond my wildest imagination. The movie *What's Love Got to Do with It* had nothing on the fight that I had with him while eight-and-a-half months pregnant.

We broke up for a few weeks, but we eventually got back together only to get evicted from our apartment when my child was five weeks old. I had not been working due to my high-risk pregnancy, and the hobby he called a job was not very profitable at the time. We eventually moved into a basement apartment I found, but two days later I made up my mind that I would not raise my child in the same abusive environment in which I had been raised.

With a negative $187 balance in my bank account, I was determined to make it on my own and provide a better life for my child. He must have seen the resolve in my eyes because he left me and the baby, taking the only bed we had to move back home with his mother, where, unlike us, he had a warm bed, food, and electricity.

The first three days after he left, I slept with the baby in my arms on the couch. I had no food, no money, and nowhere to turn. I did not eat for three days, and thank God, the baby was nursing so that she could eat. I had to wait until the food stamps came in and until I was able to pick up some food from a local food pantry. I was at the lowest point in my life and would have never imagined in a million years that I, of all people, would be there. Just a year earlier, I was on my way to medical school to become a pediatric neurosurgeon only to end up in an abusive relationship with no money and no food, as a single mother living in a basement apartment. My desperation to end the pain of heartbreak led to me making a poor relationship choice I would have never made had I given myself time to heal and get over my college sweetheart.

Although I had moved to another state with a pre-med biology degree and plans to attend medical school, I gave all of that up and eventually found a job making $11 an hour. Due to my determination and ambition, I eventually became a pharmaceutical sales rep and opened my relationship coaching firm and increased my income from $28,000 to well over six figures a year. I suffered many setbacks and challenges that could all have been avoided had I learned to a) never date while on the rebound, b) never, ever have sex with a man on the first date, and c) heal my past pain and issues before entering relationship.

The Mama's Boy

This has to be the most frustrating, annoying man — I mean guy, or maybe even boy — to deal with. This fellow has great qualities and potential but has not grown up enough yet to wean himself from nursing on his mother. Don't misunderstand me; if a man is disrespectful to his mother, he will mistreat you. However, if his mother still controls him and makes all his decisions, this is a major problem.

If his mother tells him you are not good enough for him when she has not even met you or he fails to stand up to his mother after she disrespects you, then he is a Mama's Boy and you need to rethink developing a long-term commitment with him. This guy possibly still lives with his mother beyond age 25 or would if he could because she would cook for him, clean his room, and iron his boxers if necessary. These men cannot think for themselves because their mothers have been doing it for them their entire lives. If this trait does not change in adulthood, you cannot expect it to change once you marry him. Mama's Boys are usually irresponsible, so having children with them would be your biggest mistake. They are the types who would leave you and the two kids and never look back. Save yourself the time, aggravation and the drama. RUN!

What Happened to Me: I once dated a guy who was such a Mama's Boy that he had arrested development. His mother ironed his boxers and mailed them to him on a regular basis. He was Catholic, and I was New Thought Christian, so she already didn't approve of me. Throw in the mix that I was divorced with two kids, and the woman threw a fit, demanding that her son stop seeing me. My boyfriend went from being a great guy one day to leaving me to fend for myself after a major surgery the next day. A week later, he eventually showed up and said that he couldn't be there for me because his parents were in town and his mom did not approve of our relationship. I told him that I had no time for little boys who couldn't think for themselves. This guy turned out to be a liar and a cheat with freaky sexual fantasies – most likely because he was still a little boy at heart dealing with having an overbearing mother. He was a total waste of time that could have been avoided the moment he told me his mother's opinion and that her approval meant everything to him.

The Commitment Phobic

This man recently ended a booty call affair he was having with two other women the week before he met you. Now he is ready to settle down and be with just one woman. The catch is that he has cheated or deliberately damaged every relationship that he has ever had. He has a trail of women he led to believe he loved them, but then he left. For some strange reason, you think you can change him and that he will treat you differently than he did the last 80 women. Yeah, right! He is usually hopping from job to job or city to city, really has never been in a committed relationship, and always has a reason pointing to the female for why the relationship failed. If he admits that he has had more than one girl have an abortion or has children from more than two women, then more than likely he is a Commitment Phobic man. He is a waste of time, so keep it moving!

The Romanticizer

The Romanticizer is another version of the Commitment Phobic but 10 times deadlier. These men are subtle and catch you off guard. He may be a professional man with no kids, a good job, and his own home. On the outside, he appears as if he has it going on. He is a wonderful catch on paper, but buyers beware! He is the man who loves the thrill of the chase and creating a romantic escapade that resembles something from the movies. You feel like you two are connected on every level and the lovemaking is out of this world because he pays special attention to whatever it takes to please a woman. You are now hooked. Once you are hooked, he is on the prowl for something or someone else to create another fantasy romance.

What Happened to Me: "Hey, you," yelled Terry. "How would you like a new piece of jewelry to go with those pretty eyes of yours?"

I was completely surprised and did not notice him or his jewelry booth until he asked me to check out his merchandise. Terry owned his own jewelry booth and set up shop every Wednesday on Florida State's campus and every Friday at FAMU. Over time, I looked forward to visiting Terry on Wednesday afternoons, and I even purchased a few items, just so I could experience the deep conversations we had each time. After going to the student union courtyard to see and talk with him each week, I eventually started to work with him.

At the time, Terry was like a breath of fresh air because I was depressed due to my parents' divorce after 22 years of marriage. Furthermore, my relationship with my dad was beyond strained after he cheated on my mom. Terry and I started as great friends who simply enjoyed each other's company. We talked about everything, including our former relationships, pervasive fears, and life goals. He was like an angel sent to me who lifted my spirits and showed me things I never knew or even contemplated. We had so much in common and worked well together. I did not realize that I had fallen in love with him until I missed going to see him one Wednesday, and I was distressed about it.

We dated off and on during my entire time at Florida State, and I felt as though I had discovered a love that not many were fortunate to experience. We had what some would call a storybook romance that consisted of emotions beyond any I had ever known. I could tell that these feelings scared him because he would often withdraw whenever we would get really close and experience a new level of feelings.

People marveled at our relationship because we had an amazing connection that allowed us to literally feel each other's presence if there was something wrong with the other person or if we were in the same building at the same time. When we made love, it was as if we traveled to other galaxies. We spent long hours listening to jazz, R&B, and any eclectic music that stimulated our passion.

I loved this man so much and believed that he was supposed to be my husband, but there was a dark side to our relationship. We were always breaking up. No, let me rephrase that, he was always breaking up with me. He just could not fully commit or handle the highs and lows of a relationship. Whenever I got too close and his imperfections could possibly be exposed, he would run and jump into another relationship. He continued this pattern throughout every relationship after me and left a trail of tears so long that you can probably chart the Underground Railroad by them.

I had my theories as to why this was, but one thing for sure was that although I believed he loved me very much, he had serious commitment issues that he was unwilling to resolve. After waiting for more than 13 years for him to eventually come around and see that I was meant to be his wife, I accepted the reality that I was wasting my time and deserved better.

I have spoken to countless women who have experienced almost 'magical' relationships with men who seemed to be too good to be true only to end up dumped and left with no answers. Most women fall for the trap of a Romanticizer because he catches them off guard as a friend who cares deeply. She wants to believe the excuses that he gives her for the delay in their relationship going to the next level, but unfortunately, they are just that, excuses. Understand that a Romanticizer usually has many 'friends', and he is probably sleeping with many, if not all, of them -- or wants to.

This man is so insecure that he doesn't know who he is, so a truly committed relationship scares the hell out of him because he knows you will eventually see the good, the bad, and the ugly about him. So, he jumps from romance to romance, never giving himself completely to one woman. This man will make you feel like you are destined to be soulmates one week and the next week break up with you for the smallest thing. You will find the back and forth cycle of your relationship with him dragging out for years with no end in sight. Cut your losses, Sweetheart, before he robs you of your mind, time, and heart. Let this Casanova ride himself off into the sunset far away from you and your precious time.

The Player

Women are all too familiar with this man. He is the man who thinks he is God's gift to women and that there isn't enough of him to spread around. Whenever he is caught in a lie, he has the right answer or a clever comeback. He is never satisfied with the woman he has and is always looking for better. He will look you in the eyes and lie through his teeth that you are the only woman for him. He will then leave your house, smelling like you, and tell the next woman the same thing he whispered in your ear.

I received a call from a good friend of mine one day. She told me that one of our girlfriends has a boyfriend who is now her baby's daddy but living with his other children's mother while dating my friend, who recently had his third child. A hot mess, I know but stay with me. He is also seeing her neighbor's sister down the street who is getting ready to have his fourth child. Whew! My friend further explained that he is open about who he sleeps with and threatens her that he will leave if she complains about his lifestyle! What the hell?

Many men believe that women prefer bad boys and Players, and I have asked myself this question many times. On the surface, it does appear that way when you look at movies, read novels, listen to music, or talk to some people. It seems as if bad boys are the kings of the dating jungle. They have all the girls, get laid every night, and have no ties whatsoever.

Throughout all of my interviews, it appears that although bad boys have all of the fun early in life, when they reach their later years, they find themselves alone and worn out. When they finally mature, they find that life offers so much more than superficial relationships, drunken sexapades, and drama. In the end, their emotional unavailability and desire for emotionless sex has led them down the road of never experiencing the gift of true love and the magic that finding The One can bring.

When we look at this concept from a long-term perspective, it appears that the idea that bad boys are more desirable to women is relative to age or experience. Women use bad boys to experience greater excitement, thrills, and fantasies when they are younger, but most eventually mature into preferring a good guy who is consistent, trustworthy, and doting. At least, this is the case for women who learn from their mistakes or come to realize their real worth. We all know women who never grow out of this phase and seem to prefer drama, spending their days stomping down the street in bath robes, yelling and screaming, looking for their man who never came home that night. Many women put up with this man because he usually has good game, a nice car, or his own place. Unfortunately, too many women marry this man and must bury their head in the sand in order to stay and maintain their lifestyle. It appears that these women get stuck in this type of negative relationship because they a) don't know their own worth,

b) don't know what a good man looks like, or c) think "love" is enough reason to stay with the jerk they have fallen hard for.

Ladies, the relationship choices you make today can affect your long-term happiness. If you constantly find yourself in toxic relationships and you are older than 35, then it is time to go see a professional therapist or a certified relationship coach and pay close attention to the advice I teach in this book, so that you understand the motivation for your behavior. The DIVA reading this book neither needs to settle for this kind of man nor does she need this kind of drama in her life. Put this man on the doggy train he rode in on, and don't let him forget to take his fleas with him!

The Workaholic

This man is so insecure about his manhood, height, penis size, or power that he works like a dog in order to prove to the world that he is worthy. He will put his job before you every time. He will use his job as the excuse for why he keeps breaking plans to meet, why he doesn't have time to spend with you, why he can't call at least once every other day, or why he is not ready to marry you after dating you for more than two years. No matter how high he climbs, the time will never be right because his excessive work habit is compensating for something else that he is insecure about or lacks. Do you really want to spend the rest of your life second to a job? I don't think so. Kick him to the curb, and don't look back.

I knew a woman who dated a man who worked so much that he 'forgot' to call her for weeks or even months at a time. She always gave me the excuse that he called her when "he found the time." I was sick to my stomach when I heard her story because I knew that he finds the time to do the things he wants or needs to do. He goes to the bathroom, doesn't he? I am sure he eats and watches the game. So, to believe the lie that he was just too busy to call was a delusion, and she was blind to the reality that he was not her man and just not feeling her. Men make time for what and whom they want. If the president of the United States can make time to call his wife on a regular basis, then unless her man is God, I cannot see where he is too busy to pick up the phone and spend a few minutes to see how she is doing.

There are some exceptions to this. If he is a good man who genuinely cares for you and calls you on a regular basis but has little time to spend with you or take you out, then understand that most men derive a sense of purpose from work and having a source of income makes them feel respectable. In addition, some men genuinely love you and want to provide the best for you, which is why they work so hard. If this is your situation, tell your man you would love him no matter how much money he makes and that you value his time more than the things he may give you.

Deadbeat Dads

If you are dating over the age of 30, it is likely that the men you meet will already have children. To choose to date only men with no children is your personal choice but understand that you are significantly limiting your dating options when you make this decision. Moreover, there are some great guys who happen to have kids, so I would not recommend eliminating single dads from your dating pool.

The key is to choose men who pay their child support and are active in their children's lives. If you are with a man who has children he does not speak to, see, or take care of, I would argue that he is not a good man. If you have children with this man, he will most likely do the same thing to you if your relationship with him ends. Struggling financially, especially in a bad economy, to pay his child support is one thing, but failing to communicate with his child is inexcusable. If he is uninvolved with his child while paying child support, he is still a Deadbeat Dad who is absent from his role as a father. Nothing is worse than a Deadbeat Dad, and these types of men usually have major character flaws in other areas of their lives.

Mr. Baby-Mama Drama

Most times, when a relationship ends bitterness starts, and all too often, two adults are unwilling to put their personal feelings aside in the best interest of the child and everyone involved. Some women become bitter because their ex fails to take care of their child and be a father. On the other hand, many women play the game of using their child as a pawn to get back at the ex.

Personally, I would not recommend that you date a man with children knowing that he deals with serious baby-mama drama, unless he is a great guy who is serious about you and with whom you can see having a promising future. I know the catfights and other issues may not seem appealing, but I have a few recommendations for decreasing the possibility of getting caught in a bad situation:

#1: Make sure that you are a team with ground rules for dealing with the child's mother.

When my husband and I got together, his ex-wife did not approve of me being in their child's life. She would call all hours of the day and night, instigate arguments, make unreasonable demands with the pick-up and drop-off schedule, keep him from speaking to his child, and whatever other upheaval she could conjure. The situation got ugly before it got better, but my husband and I were on the same page and created a united front in which everyone involved had to respect our relationship and our rules. There were to be no arguments over the phone, all events and conversations were documented, and phone calls before or past a certain hour were unacceptable. Eventually, she got the picture, and for the most part, she backed off when she realized we would not relent.

#2: Act like a lady and think like a child.

Especially for the child's sake, try to be pleasant with the ex as much as possible, even when she is acting immature toward you. In addition, never say anything derogatory about the child's other parent in front of the child. In doing so, the child is put in the precarious situation of either accepting or rejecting your negative comments. Think about someone talking negatively about someone you love. If you would not want something disparaging said about your mother or father, then you should avoid doing it also. Even if the child expresses discontent for his or her parent, just listen and try to be supportive without adding any further fuel.

#3: He must be willing to be a mediator.

The man must be willing to intercede if the child gets belligerent or becomes disrespectful to you. He must demand mutual respect, and not consistently or arbitrarily side with the child over you. Try to have a great relationship with the child, but if he or she does not accept you, do not go out of your way to earn the child's approval by spoiling or trying to buy the child's love. If you are consistently respectful and loving, children will come around eventually.

#4: Never ever try to discipline his child if the mother is still in the picture.

If an issue arises, tell your man and let him be the disciplinarian. You will never win on this one, and it can cause legal trouble for you and your husband. You can respectfully express your discontent and instructions for the child because you are the adult. However, if the child does something wrong that requires any type of punishment, this job should be left to the father unless you both have full custody or have been raising this child as your own since he or she was very young.

#5: Do not take your anger for the ex out on the child.

Children are innocent and have nothing to do with grown folks' drama. If anything, the situation is usually more traumatizing for the child, and they do not deserve your misdirected anger. I had to deal with major baby-mama drama, as the mother hated my close relationship with her child. She would play games and pit me against the child by saying that her child said that I said things that I didn't so that I would resent her child. She even would spank her child if the child did not reveal personal information about what went on with me and her ex. I would watch helplessly as the child endured her mother's interrogation over the phone with tears streaming down her face. This was sad and difficult to deal with, but I refused to treat the child poorly.

#6: Do not give your man a hard time about being a father to his kids.

Sometimes the situation is already hard enough as it is. Maybe he has to deal with being a part-time dad who cannot be with his kids as much as he may like. He does not need you breathing down his neck about his desire to be involved in his child's life. If you feel any type of jealousy toward his interaction with his ex, discuss this with him so he can find ways to make the situation more comfortable for you, as well as his child.

#7: Maintain a set of standards.

Just because she is the mother of his kids does not mean that she has a higher standing in his life than you. She should be well-aware of the boundaries that she cannot cross when it comes to your home and your relationship with her ex. Never approve of him, her, and the child spending family day together without you. Do not approve of him spending the night at her house. There are hotels, motels, and lodges that would welcome his visit if he needs a place to stay. Be mature and hospitable, but do not be anybody's fool!

The Pimp/Lazy Butt

We will refer to 'the pimp' as the lazy butt man we all know and may have even loved who is always "in between" jobs. He is the man who is waiting for his next big break in the music industry, his business to boom, or a sports agent to call. He does not believe in working for The Man or any man, for that matter, because he is an entrepreneur who must hang in there until his lucky break comes. Stay away from this type of man because he will suck you dry, drain your bank account, warm your sofa, and baby-sit your TV while you work your butt off to pay the bills and possibly his child support. Like a pimp, he reaps the benefits while you do all the work. Cut this lazy loser lose, and keep it moving.

The Homosexual, Down-Low Man, or Effeminate Male

This is a major issue in the African American community. JL King, author of *On the Down Low*, explains in his book how many men, afraid of the stigmas that come with being openly gay, date, have sex with, or marry a woman while being mostly attracted to men. There is not judgement here, however, these men are living a double life as a war wages inside of them to either openly be who they are or keep their sexual preference in the closet. It is unfortunate for anyone to be afraid of fully expressing who they truly are and it is my hope that as the stigma of homosexuality lifts, that the existence of men who keep their homosexuality a secret, also known as 'down low men,' decreases because there's a higher probability of HIV infection when having sex with a man who also engages in sex with other men.

If you are a Desperado (covered in Chapter 7), you will purposely overlook the signs that he is possibly homosexual or on the down low because you want a man so badly. Ladies, it is so not worth it. In fact, it is better to err on the side of caution. If he shows you any signs that he is gay or attracted to men, take off the heels and head for the hills!

One way to find out if he is sleeping with men is to just look him in the eyes and ask him. Don't ask him if he is gay; instead, ask, "Do you sleep with men?" You should be on date three to five by this point, and be prepared because he will get mad, but that's okay. Remember, you are not listening for what he says, you are reading his body language. If he hesitates and gets mad, listen to your gut, that small still voice letting you know something is wrong. If he looks you in the eye and calmly says no, this man is so straight that you can slice a sandwich with him. Cover up anyway because this doesn't mean he is 'clean'.

AIDS is a scary reality these days. I have a friend who works for the CDC who says that there are venereal diseases out there with no name or cure. Now that is frightening as hell! No matter who you are with, please cover it up and protect yourself. You will hear me say it again and again: a healthy vagina is a happy vagina, so do not do anything stupid to get her sick. Being involved with a gay man will surely increase your chances of getting Miss Thang sick.

The Man on the Rebound

This man has just gotten out of a long-term relationship and is emotionally unavailable. He is probably a great guy, but his heart is not ready. He must go through the mourning period, try to get her back, fall flat on his face, and then accept that it is finally over before he can be worth anything to you. A man on the rebound is heartbreak on a stick.

Women are very competitive and are always trying to "win" a man over, even if that means losing a piece of themselves. Don't try to fix this man because he will end up breaking your heart instead — guaranteed! Do yourself a favor and just be friends with this man until he is really ready and pursue other options in the meantime.

The Insecure Man

Men have five attributes that can cause them great insecurities. They are: his penis size, his appearance, his hair, his height, and his career or financial status.

A man with a small penis is easy to spot. He is the guy who is always talking about sex and how great he is in the bedroom. You believe the hype and go all the way with him only to find out that his penis is the size of a baby's finger, and you couldn't even tell if or when he entered you. If he never learns how to work his handicap, he will overcompensate in another area, which may annoy the hell out of you. For example, he may become a control freak, sex addict, porn freak, or pervert. Just keep your eyes open to this man.

If his insecurity is his appearance, such as being overweight, having a lazy eye, or looking like the Hunchback of Notre Dame, you really can't do much for him. He must be able to love himself first in order to love you. You do not want to spend your time trying to convince someone that they are as fine as Vin Diesel, as tall as Shaq, or that his $3 in the bank is okay with you. Let him work on his self-esteem issues and get back to you when he has gotten it together. In the meantime, keep it moving.

The Does Nothing for You Man

This is the guy who works his heart out to win you over. He seems like a great guy in every sense of the word, but he is just not the guy for you. Many women enter an unhappy relationship with this man because he is 'safe'. She has a false sense of security that this man would never cheat on her, put his hands on her, or attempt to control her. Most often, this man has no backbone and is easy to run over. He doesn't turn her on, make her heart sing, or give her butterflies. She takes her resentment for being stuck in a loveless, unfulfilling relationship out on this man by mistreating him, cheating, being apathetic, or abusive physically or verbally. The only thing that she loves about him is how much he loves her and/or her/their kids. Ladies, you can only end up in this kind of relationship if you take the easy way out and refuse to heal your stuff. This relationship is as bad as they come because it drains the life out of you and takes you further away from who God made you to be. No relationship will be full of rainbows every day, but it should at least make you feel as though you are home and that you would be satisfied if the world ended and left just the two of you. You shouldn't be watching the clock wondering how soon one of you will die, so that you can end the torture of this loveless relationship without the self-imposed embarrassment of a divorce.

Never settle – ever! Do not settle for the jerks or the good guys who just are not for you. Wait and trust God to bring you YOUR good guy and you will be a happy lady indeed.

What happened to me: Remember the story I told you about Kevin? The one-night stand, Woman Hater turned deadbeat baby daddy? Well let me refresh your memory. I was a single mother to a five-week-old. I was sleeping on a couch with my baby in my arms and no food in the house because her father (The Woman Hater) decided to take the only bed we had and move back home with his mother. I had no job and no income. He was our only source of income and he did not look back. I did not eat for three days as I waited for the food stamps and pantry food donations to come in. I was dejected and at a low when I met Larry. We met at a conference I attended where he was performing as part of a group of artists. He was very overweight, unattractive to me, but super funny. The first thing he whispered in my ear when we met was "You are going to be my wife." He pursued me for months and we eventually became friends. The thing that really drew me to him was the bond that he and my daughter instantly had. He was so loving and kind to her. He would see that I was going through a tough time and just leave diapers and groceries at my door. He wrote me poems and sang to me and boy did he make me laugh. One day I called my mother to tell her about him and how much he liked me but how I was not attracted to him at all. She told me that she didn't raise me to judge a book by its cover and that I should give him a chance.

Eventually, we kind of "fell" together because the house he and his group members were living in was sold out from under them by the label they were signed to, and he found himself homeless. He'd done so much for me that I felt obligated to return the favor and let him move in. After several months of living together our parents pressured us to get married because according to their religious beliefs we were shacking. The only problem was that I was still in love with my college love, the Commitment Phobe, and I was not attracted to Larry. I told Larry this and he was so into me that he said that it did not matter. According to him, I would eventually fall in love with him.

We held our wedding in the Bahamas and invited only our closest family and friends. As he stood at the altar, I began to walk down the aisle. At that moment, I knew I was making a mistake and turned to my bridesmaids and said, "I don't want to do this!" To their credit, they told me not to and that they would come up with something to tell our guests. With tears in my eyes I told them that he loved my daughter and was the father she didn't have and that as a mother, I couldn't take that away from her. I also felt that my guest traveled too far to see a wedding. Crazy thinking, I know but that was where I was at the time.

On our wedding night, I didn't even want to go to our room. My bridesmaids made me go to him. I spent that night in his arms crying.

For the four years that we were married, I was miserable! I did not love him and that was not changing. I also did not respect him because although he was a really sweet and funny guy, he had a problem with telling the truth and stealing. He was a kleptomaniac. People would come over our home and always "lose" the electronics that they came with. I had to pull him aside and threaten him in order for their items to magically appear between the couch cushions or under a chair. He would lie about everything, and once I secured a great paying job as a pharmaceutical representative, he magically "lost" his job while I was at training. He stayed unemployed for the last two years of our marriage. With his unwillingness to provide, control his weight gain, stealing habit, and dishonesty, I was completely turned off and did not respect him as a man. We argued all the time and I spoke to him like a dog.

I am ashamed to admit that I was a terrible person to him and there is no excuse. I spoke to him crazy in front of others and I hardly let him touch me. Yes, it is hard to admit that rainbows didn't always fly out of my heart. I had a dark side that attracted the experiences I had. I had to grow up and heal my issues. I also had to stop settling for less than what God had planned for me. We divorced a month after I found out that he was cheating on me with a tenant who lived in one of our rental properties. I had never been so happy to be cheated on in my life. Larry was not a bad guy. He still is not a bad guy even though he is a deadbeat, absent father who does bad things. Unlike Kevin, I do not believe that Larry is malicious. I just think that he has a lot of healing to do and I am thankful for the son he gave me.

The point to all this is that even though I am so thankful for the son we created, I should have never married a man I was not attracted to and did not love. Love is a *must* before you agree to marry anyone – and I am not talking infatuation. I am talking about real, love-you-when-you're-not-your-best love. You cannot manufacture love. It is not a logical process that can be reasoned into your heart. Love doesn't hurt and cause drama either, so don't deal with that in the name of love.

The Jealous Man

This type of man must know your whereabouts at all times and wants to control who you are talking to or hanging out with. They have no trust in you that you will not lie, cheat, or betray them in some way; and will give you multiple excuses and justifications for why they are jealous. More often than not, in their minds their jealousy will be your fault. Jealousy is a gateway to control and abuse. Being in a relationship with a jealous person almost never ends well and is very dramatic!

Many immature women who do not know any better initially believe that having a man who is extremely jealous is a turn on. It makes them feel as if his jealousy is a demonstration of his love and affection for her. However, there will never be a time on the face of the planet in which a woman who is with a jealous man will remain happy for the long term. There is nothing sexy, healthy, or loving about being in a relationship with a jealous person. Jealousy is a sign of a need to control. It is not a sign of love, nor is it healthy. Most often, I find that jealous people are jealous because they either are or would do something behind their partner's back (like cheating) and are afraid that their partner will, in turn, do the same to them. If you desire to die a slow death due to stress, then enter a relationship with a jealous man. It is a miserable, horrible, suffocating experience.

Don't get me wrong. Moments of jealousy in any relationship is normal. However, it should happen rarely, and should be easily cleared up with a simple conversation. Your man should give you the benefit of the doubt and you both move on to love each other another day. A jealous man always assumes the worse about your intentions and actions and seeks to control them.

If you value your sanity, safety, and happiness, stay far away from a jealous man. Jealous people are most often narcissists who are only focused on themselves and what benefits them. You cannot love this person into being a better person. You cannot ever prove to them that you are not who they think you are. He has issues that are far beyond what you can fix. He most often needs medication and psychological help. Get out while you can, as quickly as you can because being in a relationship with this kind of man can ultimately lead to death. You are not a child or someone who needs to be controlled. You are a grown woman who should be seen as an equal and treated with respect.

What Happened to Me: I will discuss this type of man in further detail when I talk about how I accidentally married a married man, but I'll talk about the abusive part of our relationship here.

There were multiple things wrong with my 'Jealous Man', whom I will refer to as JM. He initially appeared to be my knight in shining armor. He said everything I wanted to hear, gave me everything that I thought I wanted, and made me feel as though he wanted the best for me, which included an overwhelming need to protect me. Although JM acted like he was not a jealous guy during our first date, his jealous tendencies started to come out after three months of dating. If he thought I found a guy attractive, there were questions. He always had to make a comment about what I was wearing and had to know who I was talking to. I hated for my phone to ring, because that meant I would have to endure a litany of questions after the call.

I thought nothing of it when he asked me the first time who was calling my phone. I thought nothing of it when he questioned me in extensive detail about my male friends and exes. I thought the reason he insisted that we were together 24 hours a day, 7 days a week was because he enjoyed my company. I started to notice that there was a problem when he always had to know where I was going when I hung out with my friends. I didn't mind telling him, because I had nothing to hide and felt transparency in a relationship was important. However, when he would show up unannounced at the club my friends and I would be hanging out at, or had to accompany us whenever we had girls' night out, I realized that there was a problem. Whenever I would bring up an issue that bothered me, he would turn it back around on me.

This was how a typical conversation would go:

> **Me**: Why is it important that you go everywhere I go with my girlfriends?

> **JM**: What are you trying to hide? Are you trying to do things with other guys behind my back that you wouldn't do if I was there?

> **Me**: Why is it necessary whenever my phone rings that you must know who is calling me?

> **JM**: So, you do have guys calling you! Why do you think it's okay for you to disrespect me by talking to other guys behind my back?

Conversations such as these would go on and on for hours and hours almost every single day! There were times in which we would argue until 5 or 6 in the morning when we started at about 6 the evening before. I was miserable.

To make matters worse, he did not want me to work. He felt that as the man, it was his job to cover the family and provide. He was one of those types of men who insisted that I 'submit' to him. One day I will write a book on how the church has used the Bible for centuries to abuse and control women. But that is a different topic for a different day.

Since I did not work, he was the only source of income for the household. This meant that he controlled the money. Since he controlled the money, it meant that he also controlled the gas in the car and how far I could drive. He would literally time how long it took me to drop the kids off at school and if I was not back within 5 minutes of his calculated time, he would call me and insist that I remain on the phone until I got home. One time I ran out of gas because of his need to ration the gas in an effort to limit where I would drive. Since he provided and controlled the money, that meant it was my job to cook, clean, and support his golfing career. He would insist that it was my job to clean a 10,000 square foot home by myself. As the self-declared 'head of the house', he felt that it was not his job to cook or clean at all. He was very demanding and controlling and this totally worked against my personality. This meant that we fought constantly.

Just to give you an idea of how awful he was, when a family member who was significant in my life passed away, I was devastated. I did not have the money to travel to attend his funeral and JM felt that it would be a waste for me to go to a funeral for a person who was going to die anyway. As I was grieving, he rolled over in the bed and tried to have sex with me. Of course, I did not want to and the fact that I was grieving did not matter to JM. He wanted what he wanted, and he wanted it right there and then. When I said no, he launched an attack on how I wasn't doing my job as his woman and how no one should come in between our relationship not even my dead family member. He literally hollered and screamed at me for over three hours because I did not want to have sex after finding out my loved one passed away. Finally, with tears in my eyes, I complied with his wishes.

When I was a little girl, I had been inappropriately touched twice by people I knew. I never talked about how violated I felt during both encounters. That night, when JM was on top of me disregarding my grief, I felt that childhood violation all over again.

The end of the road for us came when one day we were in one of our marathon argument sessions and a friend called me. I am not sure how it happened, but her ringtone mysteriously changed to a Sade song. That immediately enraged JM and he demanded to know who was calling me. At that point I had had enough. I was done with the arguments. I was done with submitting to his wishes, his control, and abuse. When he asked to see my phone, I said no! He began to jump on top of me and tried to tackle the phone out of my hand. He hit and scratched me, but I refused to give up the phone. I was done.

JM began a tirade of calling me everything but a child of God, and I decided this time I would get a recording of his antics. At the same time, my friend called back and heard him threaten to shoot me with his gun if I did not give up the phone. When he left the room to get his gun, I ran in the closet with my friend yelling in the phone on the other end. She insisted that I call 911 and sat helplessly as she listened to her dear friend being threatened, yelled at, and verbally abused by (whom she assumed was legally) my husband.

That was the final straw. The next day I went to the courthouse to file a restraining order against JM. I discovered that day that I was in a full-fledged abusive relationship. At the courthouse, there is a department that will file restraining orders on your behalf at no cost if you are in an abusive domestic situation. They qualify you with a questionnaire in which JM's behavior checked every sign of an abuser.

I walked away from that horrible experience with $32 in my bank account, no job, and no clue how I would provide for my kids. I did believe God would make a way and God did. I could have avoided this entire situation if I'd recognized the signs of a jealous man from the beginning. I could have lost my life. I almost lost my sanity and it wasn't worth it. Ladies, even the most educated among us end up in controlling abusive relationships because it starts off slowly and you do not realize what is happening until you're in the thick of it. If you are currently in an abusive relationship, please call 1-800-799-7233 and get help.

The Married Man

DIVAs, please listen closely to me on this one. Of all the Don't Wanters out there that you need to know how to spot and avoid, the worst is the Married Man. It is an easy trap to slip into which is the reason why we need an entire chapter for this kind of man. Avoid all Don't Wanters like the plague and don't give them any excuses for their bad behavior. This is especially true for the married man. Please pay special attention in the following chapter.

Chapter 6.
Married Men

I know what you are thinking. Why would Shay create an entire chapter about why to avoid dating a married man? First, I have learned that you should never say what you would never do because life might serve a crap burger disguised as a filet mignon. Second, the ones asking this question have never found themselves in this situation and would proclaim at the top of the highest mountain that THEY would NEVER date a married man or be caught in this type of situation because only a skanky woman with a low self-esteem would ever try to break up a happy home. Well, Missy, keep reading so that you won't become a statistic.

Now don't get me wrong. Skanky, desperate women are out there who are only attracted to and pursue married men for the 'benefits' married men offer. You know the benefits I am speaking about: paid bills, trips, the thrill of the possibility of being caught, and regular sex with no strings attached. I am not judging you. I simply say that if you are this type of woman and you are reading this book, it means that you want more out of life and there are open wounds that you need to recognize within yourself and heal them.

Ladies, please understand that many unhappy, dissatisfied married men are out there who are constantly on the prowl for unsuspecting single women, especially women with children who do not know the game. We have all heard the statistics on the high rate of divorce, and these numbers are growing. This fact increases the opportunity of you being caught up emotionally with a growing population of heart-breakers. These men usually have a great woman at home who love them dearly, but for whatever reason they are unsatisfied with their marriage and searching for more. Many of the complain that their wives do not appreciate them or do not give them enough 'loving'. These men are often self-centered and unethical. They are all too ready for an easy way out when the going gets tough. Marriage isn't easy, and unhappiness does not justify cheating.

When the Married Man appears in your life, he usually has the following traits:

- He seems like a great catch
- He is charming and very convincing
- He plays the victim
- He leads a busy life
- He is great at mirroring

How It Starts

You are out somewhere, maybe with the girls and not aware that you are the next target of a lying, cheating, Married Man on the loose. When he approaches, you are caught off guard but emotionally at a place of vulnerability and can appreciate the attention. Your vulnerability may be a recent breakup, job loss, financial difficulties, a recent death in your family, or something that has triggered emotional distress. This lying buster may not even tell you at first that he is married. If he tells you he is married, he may say that he is legally separated and getting a divorce. He may even refer to his marriage as a "situation." He smells your vulnerability a mile away and knows the right things to say to spark your interest.

In the beginning, he calls you often, but probably texts you more often than he calls. When he takes you out, he is usually only available during lunch hours or before 10 p.m. and is hardly ever available to spend time with you on the weekends. If he has one of those late-night jobs or he is in the entertainment industry, he probably makes lots of late-night visits to your home on the way to the studio or a gig.

The Married Man may not even take you out at all, or he may not take you out in or near the city in which you both live. At first, you suspect that this is strange but do not really say much about this unusual dating practice. Then it happens. He goes from being all into you one day to distant the next. The calls dwindle into only text messages, and he may disappear on you for weekends or weeks at a time. As you wonder what happened, you start to panic and do everything you can to win back his affection because human nature dictates that REJECTION BREEDS OBSESSION! The more someone rejects you, the more you work to win their affection to validate your own self-worth.

At this point, you are entangled in his web of lies and locked in an emotional prison. You even believe at some point that he is YOUR man because he knows exactly what to say to create a false sense of security in your head. Finally, when your anxiety grows too high, you catch him in a lie or he is consistently inconsistent, so you try to leave the situation. Every time you attempt to let him go, he comes running back, confessing his undying love for you and pushes the right buttons to convince you to sleep with him once more. He may even tell you that he is only staying for the kids and that as soon as they turn 18, he is leaving his wife. He may even convincingly tell you that he is waiting for the right time to leave because he cannot afford a divorce because he will have to give up the house, pay alimony or child support, divide his 401K, forgo his mother's insurance policy, pay back taxes, reimburse veterinarian fees or whatever other corny excuses he can throw at you.

When you are together, he may make you feel like you are the world to him even though he has not called you in three or four days/weeks/months, etc. If you are one of the unfortunate women who end up in this type of situation, you will find that during the holidays, 'your' man, although separated, is nowhere to be found and is even too busy to call you. This includes News Year's Day, President's Day, Labor Day and even Valentine's Day. Although you often question him, and your instincts tell you to leave him, you find that it hurts too badly to stay but it hurts worse to leave. The rockets are blazing and the red flags are flapping to declare that the man you're in love with is married and belongs to someone else, but you are stuck between the guilt and the desire to believe the lies that he is feeding you.

How It Ends

His game is a classic trap that easily causes even the smartest of women to slip.

Please understand that no matter how great this man appears to be, no matter how great the sex is, no matter how much of a bitch he says his wife is, no matter how often he says that he is going to leave, and no matter how much he says that he loves only you, sleeps with only you, and wants to spend the rest of his life with only you, the entire relationship with you is a lie! You fell in love with a lie. The relationship is built on a lie, and that man, who is NOT yours, is a selfish liar. He is cheating because he can get away with it and the truth is that you are allowing it. If he can lie and cheat on the woman he promised before God to love and cherish, forsaking all others until death do us part, then what makes you think that he is being completely honest with you?

Many men reveal that they do become attached to the other woman and come to need the other woman as much as they need their wives. The problem is that the wife gets all of him while you, his mistress, get her sloppy seconds. The relationship that he has with his wife is real. She sees him snore, washes his dirty underwear, deals with his mood swings, goes through financial challenges with him, sees him cry, talks to his mother, goes to church with him every Sunday, raises their kids with him, and even accepts his unfaithful ways — that is another book. Of course, they are going to have issues. You would have issues too if you were married to a lying, cheating, unethical, selfish man like that. He is using you as his release or a retreat on the side as he temporarily runs from his real life.

Say it with me: You are the other woman! I know this is harsh but some of you are really stuck in this purgatory and need a good kick in the butt to get out. He is clearly a Nacho, or Not Your Man. No matter how great or connected you think you are, he is not, will not, could not, should not, and will not ever leave his wife for you. Even if he did, do you really want a man who cheated on someone else? I know some of you are still in this foggy dream world, jumping up and down shouting at the book saying that YOUR situation is different. He really loves you and is going to leave his wife for YOU, and I don't know what I am talking about. Well, first, let me say that no matter how loud you yell at me, I cannot hear you! Second, if you want your ovaries to go hard-boiled while you wait on this two-timing loser, then you go right ahead, but you had better pray that he does not leave her and marry you because I can guarantee with mathematical certainty that he will do the same thing to you with someone else. Oh, so you think you are so off the chain that he would never do the same to you. Suppose you get this man but have no peace of mind, knowing that karma is a bitch. I don't think you want to be constantly looking over your shoulders when you do get married because you stole someone else's man.

The bottom line is: married is married. I know in this new age, fewer people respect the sanctity of marriage. This fact has even allowed us to drop our guard about dating while separated with no divorce papers filed. One woman dated a separated man for 10 years. He was really good to her and her kids. Her family even loved him, and he supposedly loved the lady dearly. When his wife got sick, he left the lady and went back to take care of his wife. Ten years later, he and his wife are still married and living together.

For single woman with children, do you really want to take this chance and allow this kind of drama in your kids' life? Children have their own set of challenges, and do you want to add the issues that come with dating a married man to their lives as well? Do you really want to spend lonely nights crying from a broken heart?

Every woman I have polled who has ever been involved with someone married, separated, or in a 'situation' has always ended up heartbroken. I know many of you have stories of how it can work or how a co-worker whose cousin's sister knows of a man who left his wife for the other woman and how they lived happily ever after. Those stories, however, are rare exceptions, and give the story a little more time to play out.

What Happened to Me: I fell head over heels for this grey-eyed deejay named DJ Sexy L, and he was every bit of that. He had a way with the turntable that would hypnotize people. He was one of the best DJs I had ever heard because he had a way of taking you on a trip emotionally with his skills. The night we met, I didn't notice that he was watching me as I did my Tampa booty twerk dancing.

The moment he walked up to me, I felt electricity throughout my body. Bells all went off in my head, but a voice within told me to run. I wanted to run, but I couldn't because he was extremely gorgeous with sexy eyes. I was hooked from the first moment he entered my energy field. He had so much swagger and personality. There was so much more to him than the stereotypes that are associated with DJs. He was smart and well-rounded, making me think as much as he made me laugh.

We danced and moved together as if we knew each other for years. When he asked me for my phone number that night, I told him no because I tried to listen to the voice. The following month, I saw him again, and he turned up the heat. We danced some more, and he made my stomach ache with his jokes. I stayed at that party until the music stopped because he asked me to hang around so that we could talk. I couldn't help but to take him up on that offer. After we talked and laughed for a while, he asked me if we could hang out sometime. It was getting late and security was throwing me out, so I told him to find me on *MySpace* (this should give you an idea of how long ago this was), and we would go from there.

I could not stop myself from thinking about him. It was absolutely crazy, almost as if an invisible magnet drew me into him. When two days went by and I didn't hear from him, I should have gotten the hint then, but I was in a fast car headed for a wall and just couldn't get out of the vehicle. When he finally requested that I add him as a friend, I was so excited. We started talking and planned our first date on a golf course.

At this point, I still did not know that he was married. I asked him if he had any kids, and he said no. I then tried to start a conversation about his personal life, but he seemed very tight-lipped, as if he was keeping a secret. The date was terrible because he had the nerve to make me pay for myself, a fact he later disputed. Also, he spent the entire time texting, and for all those who have listened to my advice over the years, you know I hate that. I strongly dislike texting as a main form of communication while dating; and I am turned off by people who lack text etiquette. It is very rude to text while at dinner or on a date. More about that later. Lastly, he tried to kiss me on our first date when I didn't even really know him like that. I was annoyed, to say the least, and did not answer his call for a month.

I still had him on my mind although not as strongly as when we met, so I did a *Google* search. I discovered on one of his profiles that he was married. I figured that it had to be false because he never wore a ring, aggressively pursued me, and tried to kiss me. I was so naive.

The next time that I saw him at the same monthly party, I asked him if he was married. He said yes but going through a divorce. I said well once you handle that, come talk to me. I started to walk away, but he grabbed my arm. He said that he was in the process of handling his situation and wanted to see where "we" could go, as he stared deep into my eyes with his beautiful grey eyes. He told me that he was not even living with her. Ignorantly, I took his words at face value because I, too, went through a separation while getting a divorce, so I understood what it was like to end a marriage. He also took me to the place where he was staying, his friend's basement, and I could easily tell that he was living there.

I never intended to have sex with the gorgeous, grey-eyed DJ who made my heart melt whenever he looked at me or touched me. I liked him but still kept some safe distance. One night, I was hanging out with this other narcissistic jerk that kept trying to kiss me. He was short, wealthy, and drove a nice car, but he was very pushy. I didn't like him at all and had enough of him. He got mad at me when I told him that I had to be home by 10 p.m. and told me to forget about the date because he could drop me off now. I told him not to worry about dropping me off at my car because I could get home by myself. And with that, he drove off. I was near one of my favorite hangout spots, so I walked in and ordered a drink. I am not a drinker, so I started to feel tipsy after only a few sips.

Feeling light-headed, I needed to figure out how to get home. I called a few friends and some associates, but I could not reach anyone to come and take me home. I scrolled through my phonebook, and when I came to the DJ's name, I sent him a text. At this point, he and I had not hung out in over two months, nor had we talked on the phone often. Because of our instant connection, however, I felt very comfortable contacting him. When I came across his name, I sent him a text asking him if he was busy. I told him that I was stranded and needed a ride home. He picked me up within an hour. Instead of taking me home, he told me that he wanted to show me something and took me to the waterfalls at a really nice park.

We stood there using very few words because in my right mind, I felt I should have walked home instead of contacting him, but I felt electricity that compelled me. It was almost as if I was possessed. I knew that I should not be there with him no matter what he said about his situation. I abandoned my morals because the truth is that I hated myself. At the time, my father and I weren't getting along, and I hated myself for being a single mother. This life was not supposed to happen to me. I was educated and pretty, but still, I had fallen for the games men play and had a hard time finding a good guy.

Many women look at me and ask how I can give relationship advice when it should be so easy for me to succeed in dating and relationships. They feel that I am beautiful and should not have to struggle. I would just shake my head and say to myself, "If only you knew." Good guys with good intentions are often too intimidated to approach an attractive woman, so that oftentimes leaves the arrogant guys with bad intentions. Attractive women struggle with their love life like anyone else and maybe even more so. Most men are visual and go after women with the intention of sex, so they are willing to turn up the charm and say anything to get a woman in bed. Most women are auditory and do not place more weight on a man's actions than his words. What ultimately happens is that he works hard enough to get her in bed and she hears enough great things from him that her emotions get the best of her, and she lets her guard down too soon and opens her heart, mind and body to the man she trusted and believed meant what he said to her prior to jumping in bed with him.

Had I not had a couple of drinks and was in my right mind, I would probably not have entertained sleeping with him. That night, my mind had been somewhat altered and my inhibitions had been lowered from drinking. I shrugged off the fact that he was still married because he was working on his situation. This was just an excuse to justify acting on what I fought feeling for so long.

I was never a big drinker, nor had I ever smoked marijuana or done any other kind of drugs, but this man was my own personal brand of crack. I was addicted even before we had sex, and I didn't know why. Every time he touched me or stood near me, I would almost faint. My heart would race, and an instant rush of adrenaline would pulsate through my veins. I had never felt that feeling before, and I didn't know how to control it. Had I known then what I know now, I would have run. I'll explain later how these feelings are a demonstration of your subconscious mind recognizing a potentially dangerous situation that may bring emotional harm or distress.

He took me to my car, which was parked in a shopping center parking lot about 10 miles from my house. Since I was still tipsy, he asked me if I wanted him to follow me home to make sure I made it safely. I didn't answer him the first time he asked, but then he asked again, and I didn't say no. When we pulled up to my home, he stepped out of his car and gave me the most amazing hug. I was now really horny because it had been five months. I walked to my door and he stood right behind me. I introduced him to the sitter, paid her, and then she left.

The first time we had sex, it was just that: sex. I didn't really feel that it was amazing. I rationalized that I was having innocent fun. I knew that he would never be my husband, so I should expect no emotional attachment. I was so wrong. We eventually developed a friendship. He called me every day, invited me to workout with him and his friends, treated me like I was his girl, and supported me when I needed him. He asked me to be his girl by the third time we made love, and I gladly accepted, pushing aside the thought that he was already married – albeit, getting a divorce but still married. It wasn't until the phone calls dwindled into sporadic text messages, the visits went from daytime to late-night drop-ins, and the dates became disappointments in which he started standing me up, that I began to realize that I was in over my head. It was then I started to question what was really going on with his "situation."

The breaking point came when he didn't visit me for Thanksgiving and did not even call or answer my call. I did not hear from him for two weeks after that. I was devastated, hurt and confused. Then one day, he sent me a text message. I didn't respond, so he called and told me that he had to talk to me in person. He told me that he was having a hard time with the divorce and just found out that his wife was pregnant, but the baby was not his. I felt so sorry for him and could imagine how painful that must have been for him, so I backed off and told him to take his time. I figured that he needed my support, not my demands during this time. I was fooling myself because when a man cares about you, a) he doesn't disappear on you, b) he will prove to you that you are the person he wants, and c) his words and actions will not contradict each other.

❤

Christmas and New Year's Eve came around, and he was unavailable again because he said he had DJ gigs. I was patient until he told me on New Year's Eve at 11:57 p.m. that the baby his wife was carrying might be his and that he did not know if he wanted to leave her. I entered the New Year crushed. I finally broke things off with him a month later, on the day I found out via text that his son was born. When I was not with him, I was miserable and cried daily from the depth of my soul. I could not talk to anyone about it because I was ashamed; and at the time, praying did not make me feel better. I was really doing well for a few months until he called me out of the blue and asked to stop by my home to talk. I missed him and could not resist the urge to see him.

When he arrived, I told him that I couldn't see him anymore and was not breaking up his home. I also shared with him that I realized that he was back with his wife and that continuing like this would affirm that I was alright with dating a married man who had a family. I was angry with him for lying to me, and the hurt was apparent from my somber expression. He attempted to convince me that his marriage was over, that he filed for divorce and had moved out. He begged me to be patient with him as he told me over and over again that he wanted only me. I did not believe him. I was done.

He stood up in front of me and my body crumbled again. I was paralyzed as he started to kiss and touch me. When we made love, we both cried. I think that he knew, as I did, that we were over, and this would be the last time we would be together.

When I broke things off for good, he asked me why, and I told him because I had to save my life. I hated myself for what I was doing to his wife, and every day, I prayed for her forgiveness. I do not project blame on only him. I am no one's victim. I had a choice and could have maintained my morals, but I rationalized the situation and paid dearly for it later.

Walking away from him was one of the hardest things that I ever did. I had a dream one night that I met his wife and spoke with her.

She told me that she wanted her marriage to work and for her new son to have his dad around him. I promised her in the dream that I would walk away. I also asked her for her forgiveness. I then had a dream that showed my death if I continued the relationship with him. I know that it sounds dramatic, but the situation was dramatic.

Two weeks after breaking up with him, I suffered a minor heart attack. I eventually learned that after our break up, he filed for divorce and the marriage ended. I have been asked if I regret not waiting it out, and I say no. I am glad that I left before the divorce because I was miserable, he was forced to make a genuine decision, and I wanted my own man.

Although we started out just casually, our relationship evolved into more than that because we fulfilled each other's most urgent needs. Not all affairs with a married man are just about sex and deception. Some affairs generate strong emotional attachments. However, at the end of the day, if a married man has to choose between you and his wife, he will typically choose his wife because she is the one he protects, supports, and fell in love with before you.

Dating a married man is like driving a car off a cliff. If I can help other women avoid this fate, my experience was worth the pain. My heart hurt so bad that it almost killed me. I crawled my way back to life, and it took a lot of work to get over that experience. I eventually forgave myself and used that experience for my betterment and have shared that hard-earned wisdom with others. Whenever a married man attempted to date me, I immediately turned him down. My new motto was "I am allergic to married men," and I really had an aversion to them. I was so offended whenever a married man approached me that I would get sick to my stomach. Karma is really tough – I believe that I eventually reaped what I had sown by unknowingly marrying a married man who was extremely deceiving, insecure, and abusive, as you read about in the Jealous Man section of this chapter and will learn more about in Chapter 10.

♥

If you have found yourself in this situation, forgive yourself and get out. Many good, moral, intelligent women find themselves in this easy trap. Leave these lying, cheating, time wasters alone and find a man of your own. There are no exceptions to this one. Keep it moving before it even starts and save your heart the trouble.

Chapter 7.
The Ivy League

All heterosexual males who date women desire sex. Males are naturally driven to do whatever it takes to attain sex from the object of their attraction. Don't let them fool you on this one! If he doesn't want sex from you, he is possibly homosexual, asexual, or has a nonexistent sex drive that will be very dissatisfying in the future. If he is attracted to men and you are a heterosexual woman, didn't I tell you in Chapter 5 to run like hell in the other direction? My DIVAs don't need these kinds of problems!

You are on the journey to attracting a MAN! A man is not controlled by his lower extremities. He is driven by his higher understanding of who he is and Whose he is. He is a man of God who is looking for his soulmate and he takes this job very seriously. I will be upfront and honest with you. These men do exist but the quality of them increases with age. There are too many men above 27 who are still operating as boys. Do not be fooled by age. Pay attention to consistent actions. Most young males (between 18- 27) are driven by the natural urge to have sex. Keep this in mind and act accordingly.

So now that you know this, don't go telling every man you meet: "All you want from me is sex," or "All men want is sex." Don't let him know that you know his motivation. Just store this information in the back of your head and use it to get the man you want. Now pay attention, because this information will put you in the Ivy League, where only the best students get selected and graduate successfully onto the next level.

Warning: These rules may come off as strong and harsh. I base these rules from scientific research and surveys from men. In these surveys I included questions that asked them what turns them on and off about the opposite sex. If you are still single and want love, follow these recommendations because the fact is that what you are doing is not working. These rules are not to judge you or make you feel bad but to help you feel good about you. Feeling good about yourself will radiate through you making you an irresistible catch. Taking care of yourself sends a message that you love yourself and that whoever attempts to come into your world must be willing to treat you with care. Here are basic rules to learn before proceeding:

Rule #1: Look Good

Men desire a woman who will turn him on physically and mentally. You catch a man's attention with your sex appeal and keep his heart with your whip appeal — mental, that is. Men are visual, so please remember that the next time you enter a committed relationship and attempt go to bed with him EVERY night wearing unflattering bed clothes and a sleep cap during sex.

I am not saying not to be comfortable most nights. I am saying to make a conscious effort to be sexy for your man on a regular basis. Commit to wearing a sexy teddy once a week at least, if wearing lingerie is not your thing. Take off your silk sleep cap during love making if you wear one regularly to protect your beautiful curls. Single women, please do not go out to the grocery store looking like who did it and what the hell! When you feel good, it is a turn on that will keep him wanting more of you...all of you.

His attraction for you starts with his eyes and then works its way down to his heart. Just pay close attention to the following chapters, and you will master the secrets of capturing a man's heart both mentally and physically.

Rule #2: Smell Good

In the wild, animals use their natural pheromones to attract the opposite sex. Humans are no different. There is a fine line between turning a man on with your sweet aroma and knocking him down with your tiger pheromones. If your perfume can be detected 10 minutes after you have left the room, then you have used too much. The scent should be soft and subtle, just slightly noticeable. Ask your friends and family to be honest with you about your perfume. I recommend natural lotions and oils. They are soft, fragrant, and a turn on for men. If you decide to use perfume, avoid spraying it directly on your body, or it may be overkill. Try spraying it in the air and walking through the mist.

Rule #3: Dress Nice

This one is really going to be a surprise to some women, but men do NOT care if you paid $10 or $100 for your top or your shoes. All that matters to them is how sexy and classy you look in the clothes you wear. Remember that throughout the years, styles will change but what will always remain the same is that LESS IS MORE! There is a fine line between dressing sexy and dressing like a street walker. When you dress like a wife, you are more likely to be seen as one. This has been scientifically proven. A study was done in which pictures of scantily dressed women and women who wore sexy yet classy clothing were presented to male-only test subjects that were hooked up to brain monitors. Each time the scantily dressed pictures appeared on the screen, the part of the brain that recognizes inanimate objects lit up. Every time pictures of women dressed in a classier way flashed across the screen, the part of their brain that associates with humanization lit up. This means that men subconsciously objectify scantily dressed women. In their minds, these women were good for sex only, not marriage. If your reproductive organs including nipples, full butt cheeks and breast can be seen through your clothing, you are doing way too much and need to rethink your clothing choice. If you are a beautiful, plus size woman, please wear clothes that fit and flatter your body. Love your body and all your curves and show this by wearing garments that make you feel confident and beautiful. If we can see each and every roll that you are working with under that very tight-fitting dress, that dress is the wrong choice. Even if it is the style, it is not stylish on you. I am a firm believer in Spanx for every woman of any size. It smooths and shapes and helps you to carry your head up much higher and yourself with much more confidence. Get a pair asap! Remember, NOT all outfits look good on *every* body. Stop dressing like the women in the videos and start buying clothes that look nice on your body. Please make sure that you find your style and work it.

Rule #4: Wear Makeup, Please!

Some of you believe that you look better *au naturel*. I do not care what Alicia Keys says, there is a time and place to wear makeup and the Red Carpet is definitely one of those places – but that's a different story. Do not let an already-married celebrity creating a brand mess you up when you are working on attracting your future mate! You may have beautiful skin and nice kissable lips, but a little makeup will only enhance them. Makeup brings out those great features, such as your eyes, that men like so much. Do not overdo the makeup; you don't want to be mistaken for a call girl or a drag queen. The men I interviewed during my research revealed that they prefer women who are beautiful while wearing a natural looking makeup. Put on just enough to even the skin tone, accent the eyes, play up those sexy lips, and cover those blemishes. Make the time to amplify you!

Eyelashes: Wear natural looking eyelashes! Wearing eyelash extensions are not a must-wear in my book if you can simply use mascara to accent your eyelashes. I am adding a few comments about eyelashes because false eyelashes or eyelash extensions have become very popular and more women are wearing them. With that has come too many women who are overdoing it and wondering why they are still single. Ladies, the goal is to enhance your assets while looking as natural as possible. If your eyelashes look like fanned out fingers, then you are doing way too much! If someone can see the glue that connects the lash strip to your eyelid, this is not cute! Please wear these beautiful eye enhancers gracefully.

Rule #5: Shave

This applies to all areas other than the head. Shave your legs because legs that look like Bigfoot's under arms are not considered cute in the United States. Wax your upper lip if it needs it. Please eliminate the unibrow, which went out with the caveman. Pluck those eyebrows, your chin, and chest hairs. For Heaven sake, please shave under your arms regularly because nothing looks worse than a cute girl who lifts her arm and a tree pops out! Also, don't forget to take care of your bikini line. I know there are many thoughts around keeping up the bikini line and I know that it itches when it is shaved and hurts like a mother flipper when it is being waxed. Try to have an open mind. Many men I surveyed stated that they find it sexy when a woman keeps up her bikini line. If you want to please your man while turning yourself on, please take care of this area. Many men like it trimmed up and Brazilian waxed, not bald or bushy.

Rule #6: Be Fun

Every man wants a woman he can have fun with, but he still wants her to remain a lady, and of course, he wants to have great – not just good – sex with her as well. We will talk more about the sex part in Chapter 15. Many women are walking around with attitudes so sour that even Jesus wouldn't approach. Resting bitch face may spare you wrinkles but there will be no point if you are left old and single for the rest of your life. Some women think that acting standoffish and rude makes them more desirable to men. News flash, Sweetheart, no man wants to deal with a bitter, angry woman who is always complaining or nagging him about something.

I will continue to assert: forgive, heal and let go of your pain because it is only standing in the way of your happiness. In fact, put a smile on your face when you get up in the morning and wear it throughout your day and you will be surprised how many compliments you get and how many more men approach you.

♥

Rule #7: Watch Your Words

Most men are afraid of committing to the wrong woman. When he first meets you, he doesn't know if you are the right woman or not; so, hold off for at least the first month from talking about marriage, love, more kids, puppies, your therapist, and meeting the parents. Some of you ladies are moving much too fast. SLOW DOWN. Love does not happen overnight.

Give the relationship time to build a true foundation of friendship and allow yourself time to determine if he is who he says he is. On the other hand, it doesn't take a man forever to determine if he wants a relationship with you. Nor does he need a profusion of years to know if he wants to marry you. Men are simple. Either he is feeling you or he isn't. If he doesn't want to commit to you, let him go.

But back to your words. Don't kill your chances of a potentially great relationship with a great guy by opening your conversation saying, "How many children do you want?" Be discreet and patient, allowing the relationship to progress while keeping your eyes open to any potential signs that he is a Don't Wanter or just not feeling you.

Ladies, I also recommend that if you have a potty mouth, clean it up! It is not ladylike or classy at all and can be a turn off to both men and women. Use your words to create – not destroy – and aim to have positive words, in the total sense, come out your mouth.

Rule #8: Make the Right First Impression

Most men have consciously or subconsciously placed you into a category and timed how long they project the relationship will last before you have even said, "Nice meeting you." After he has approached you, had a conversation, and gotten your phone number, he knows for sure in which category he will place you. He will also decide the first time he meets you if he would marry you or take you home to meet his mother. You get to determine which category you will be placed in by your appearance, the way your carry yourself and your actions. Here are the categories:

The Desperado (1 night to a few weeks)

This desperate, insecure woman doesn't know her worth and *has* to have a man. These women are easy to spot because they wear that disgusting perfume called *Desperate*. They usually dress tacky, get sloppy drunk, grope or feel all over a man, and talk and laugh loudly to be noticed by any man or woman, for that matter, who will give them some attention. Men know that this girl is easy and will not put up a fight when they try to get in her pants. She is nowhere near girlfriend material let alone marriage material. Even if you are desperate, which many of us have been after having our hearts broken and landing in the rebound phase, do not, under any circumstances, show it to the world. Ask your guy friend how you appear to a man or how you may be perceived by others. If you feel yourself badly wanting to be next to a warm body to numb the pain of lost love, lust, or infatuation, please stay home instead, rent a movie, call some friends over, and just have a girl's night in. The desperate girl is easy to get and manipulate, and she always gets the Don't Wanters.

The Free Vagina Giver (1 day to 2 months)

This woman is much worse than the Desperado. She is not only desperate, but she uses her vagina as currency to buy the affection of a man she wants. She does not require that the man commit to her. For some of these women, a simple dinner will do and then she jumps in bed with a man like a 9-year-old in a pillow fight only to wake up the next morning hurt because he left without a note, never to call her again. Some of these women believe that because of the sexual revolution, men are more accepting of a sexually liberated woman and will appreciate her more than the hard-nosed DIVA who keeps her legs closed throughout the dating process.

When I was in college, I had three extremely close friends. The four of us hardly ever went anywhere without the other three. We often compared ourselves to the women from *Sex and the City* and laughed about our personality similarities with the characters on the show. Like Miranda Hobbes, one of my girlfriends dressed professionally every day, acted more mature than the rest of us. She was considered the "serious one" who was a self-declared undercover freak. Another friend, like Charlotte York, was considered the "hopeless romantic" who was constantly searching for true love while approaching life and love like one huge playground. My last girlfriend, like Samantha Jones, was sexually liberated and slept with whomever she chose. Still, she was also the one who always seemed to choose the wrong guys, and she found this out only after she slept with them. I was the advisor of the circle and had a reputation on campus for being the "hard-to-get, over-achieving" girl. Similar to Carrie Bradshaw on the show, I spent the majority of my college years in a relationship and advising other women on relationship issues.

We truly represented a full spectrum of approaches to dating and relationships. While all of us sometimes made not-so-great decisions, the friend who consistently had the worse experiences was the one with the "Samantha complex," who mistook her sexual freedom for power. Like many fans of *Sex and the City*, my friend fell victim to the sex-is-power complex and came up disappointed after every sexual escapade. Ladies, just because Samantha seemed to have it all and stay emotionally detached from the men she bedded, does not mean that this is a realistic ability most women can maintain. I am uncertain whether my friend's behavior was a result of her childhood experiences or her habitual worship of shows like *Sex and the City*. However, what is certain is that after she has had triple digit partners, three children, and now a live-in boyfriend of several years, she, at age 42, has yet to be married and would admit to anyone that she is unhappy about her past relationships and poor choices.

Millions of single women tuned into *Sex and the City* to discover who Samantha was going to sleep with each week. Watching Samantha jump in and out of bed with different men decreased the sexual restraints of single females all over the country who attempted to mimic her behavior. Samantha's character glorified being a slut, and women forgot or even dismissed the fact that no matter how 'sexually free' they may have thought they were, men would always judge a woman based on her actions and treat her based on the value she placed on herself. Women threw caution to the wind and dismissed the fact that men will have sex with easy women without restraint but marry good girls with discretion.

I have a secret that will take you a long way. If you want a man to take you seriously and give you more than he has given any other woman, keep your legs closed and focus on setting his heart on fire for you! If you have been sexually indiscriminate up to this point, remember, life is like one big university, offering enlightening lessons based on our choices. We can learn from our past mistakes and earn a badge of wisdom to create a better experience today. One's past performance is never indicative of one's future possibilities.

The Youngster (3 months to 2 years)
This is the young, wet behind the ears, recent graduate. This woman is new to the scene of real-world dating or relationships. She has gotten her diploma or degree and is officially independent. She is on her way to success and believes in the fairytales she sees in the movies of love at first sight. The downfall is that the young men who are also new to the world of independence are like kids in a candy store. They are also new to their own money, power, and real-world understanding, but they are looking to sow their oats. The Youngster female can still find love with a Youngster male, but she must make sure that she keeps this in the back of her mind so that she doesn't waste her time or end up hurt by one of these free-floating birds. Never put too much pressure on these types of guys too soon to make a commitment (i.e., the first five weeks) because they will run the other way faster than you can say the word "fidelity." Recognize when a young man is not looking to settle down and keep it moving. You will know the difference because he will say that he wants to commit to you after dating for a few months verses the man who says that there is no reason to

put a label on the relationship. No label means no commitment and no commitment means that he can and is exploring his options.

The Overly Religious (0 months to 0 years)

I have never met more single, frustrated women than the Overly Religious women. I know that some of you 'holy rollers' want to stone me right now, but before I get started, I will just ask that you breathe and have an open mind and heart. I meet many single church-going women with their Bibles in one hand and their judgments in the other. They tell me that Jesus is the number one man in their life and they need no one else. They also say that when God is ready, He will bring a man into their lives, even though they go nowhere and do nothing fun for themselves but pray, read the Bible, attend church, and go to work.

I am not hating on you. I love God with all of my heart and know that I have a direct relationship with my Papa God. I believe that God is the source of all life and infinitely powerful. It is important that we are constantly plugged into and connected to this power source not just with ritualistic actions but with our hearts. Unfortunately, many women are allowing their religious rituals or maybe their dogmas, to cause them to get played – or even worse – left alone.

These women are conflicted because, on one hand, they want a man, but on the other hand, their religious doctrines are blocking them from being able to attract and keep a man. If you spend all your extra time in the church, you are at a disadvantage. Statistics show that fewer single men attend church compared to single women. Other men, especially the alpha males, have a hard time submitting to another man, even if it is the pastor, because a man's natural inclination is to lead and be the most admired man in his home. Watching his lady admire and almost worship another man, such as the pastor, is a bitter pill, so many men intentionally avoid the Overly Religious woman.

In addition, many religious women demand that they not only find a Godly man who goes to church, but he must also be a Godly man who goes to *her* church and desires to attend service every day of the week like they do. They praise and worship God, revere the pastor, but come home and disrespect their men under the excuse that "God comes first, and I do not have to focus on pleasing you so long as I please my God!" I cannot emphasize enough that *significance* is a major need for most men. A man must feel as though you respect him, love him and appreciate him as much as you do your church and your pastor.

Additionally, many frustrated, Overly Religious women use religion to hide their cloak of hurt, fear, or shame, never really facing their issues but rather covering them up with their religious dogmas. On top of that, many radical believers have never really forgiven themselves or healed from their self-condemnation after doing things in their past that they are ashamed of or regret. Instead, they mask self-loathing with the appearance of love and fervor for the Lord. Until you heal those issues and limiting beliefs, love will continue to evade you because your hurt will continue to send the signal that you are unreceptive to love or unlovable.

Also, many excessively religious women have so many rules that they either cannot date at all; or if they do date, they cannot date a man if he is not in the church, perfect, or Godly. What about the men who believe in God but who need you to help them to see God through you and in you? It may be the hem of your garment that they may need to touch in order to have God and His will for them revealed through you.

Nothing is wrong with dating. The goal is to get out and meet men so that you are in position to meet more options. If more women date instead of marrying the first man that they are sexually attracted to, maybe less women would find themselves in unhappy marriages of abuse, cheating, and power struggles. Dating does not have to involve sex. There are men out there who are willing to wait to have sex if that is your standard, but you have to know how to present your unwillingness to have sex before marriage without coming off as though you are condemning him if he desires to have sex before marriage. You do not have to announce your unwillingness to "fornicate" on the first date. Every conversation with him does not have to be a repeat of a sermon. Sit back and relax and let the God within you shine through you because it is your light that will come off way more attractive than anything you try to convince him that you are.

I do not recommend that you compromise your standards and your beliefs by having sex, hanging out at clubs, or cursing like a sailor. As a matter of fact, I am strongly against all of the above, but I do recommend that you be open and lower your critical, judgmental criteria enough to identify a good man who may not be perfect or very religious but who may want to do better and be with your beautiful God-fearing self.

The High Maintenance (1 week to a month)

Most men accuse the High Maintenance girl of being a gold digger. They are usually dressed in very expensive clothing, gaudy jewelry, and lots of makeup with their noses in the air and their weaves down their back. These are the Paris Hiltons, video vixens, and the ballplayer-girlfriend wannabes. Many of these women are simply over-confident because of their outside beauty. I call this the "Beautiful Woman Dilemma" because many attractive women remain unmarried and have a hard time attracting a healthy relationship because they get caught in the trap of their beauty. Most guys will not even approach this girl for fear that they will be shot down or have their bank account drained within the first six months of the relationship. The men who will approach her are usually Players (see chapter 5) and will want to sleep with her but will not think about a long-term relationship. Men with money avoid these women like the plague because they fear having their credit ruined and bank accounts drained by trusting a big butt and a smile.

I receive emails at least once a week from some beautiful, High Maintenance girl who wants to know why she can't find a good man or why a man she loves so much keeps breaking her heart. I answer by saying that if you place all your value on your outer appearance, you will lose every time because men are first attracted to what visually stimulates them. When they see what they want, they are willing to say and do anything to get it. Many women love to hear the right words even if it is not followed up by the right actions. What happens is that this woman hears what she likes and lowers her guard and has sex too soon with the wrong guy. He leaves or does not pursue her as he once did, and her self-esteem is now in the toilet. If she instead placed more value on her intelligence, character, or who she is as a child of God, she would not settle for cheap talk or a man who clearly wanted to use her for sex. She would let him know her standards up front and if he could not deliver, she would hold her hand up and say, "NEXT!"

The Stuffy Uptight (1 month to a few years)
This is the girl who may have about ten college degrees on her wall, a Bible under her arm, and a few bones in her closet. She is so uptight that she wouldn't notice a man flirting with her if he sat on her head. She has strict rules for how a man should approach her, have sex with her, and be her man. She is often pursued because men love a challenge, but this woman is usually strung along because her pride will not allow her to let go of a no-good loser when he shows her that he is unworthy. She is the woman he loves to chase, but once he catches her, she is tossed aside like yesterday's salad. He will get all he can get from this woman and then sabotage the relationship so that she breaks up with him to be with the DIVA he really wants.

The Cool One of the Guys (0 months to 0 years)
You are probably wondering why this girl would have a hard time getting her man to commit to her. Although she is cool to hang out with and his friends can have a drinking contest with her, she is the girl that is eventually pushed into the good friend position or constantly hears, "I see you as a little sister or one of the guys." She is always surrounded by men, so when men see her, they do not approach her. She might cuss like a sailor, belch like a dude, or drink like a camel. She is so cool that she loses her femininity and is no longer viewed as an option to the men around her. Real, straight

men want a woman to adore, they do not want to date another dude.

The DIVA (6 months to Forever)

The term 'diva' has a negative connotation but the DIVA we discuss fits none of the stereotypes of a diva. DIVA stands for Divine, Intelligent, Vivacious and Alluring (I discuss this in detail later). She knows who and Whose she is as a child of God. She is career-minded, has her own life, and a man is just an added, desired bonus. She is not ashamed to admit that she desires love and is willing to put in the work to attract the right and perfect love experience for her. She is the girl with so many men knocking at her door that she doesn't have the time or energy to attend to them all. She is selective and never settles for a relationship that doesn't feel right. A DIVA uses the Law of Attraction to attract the man that God has already selected for her. She values her body enough not to pull down her panties after only three dates. She knows her self-worth, so when she sees a guy trying to play games, she is quick to kick him to the curb. This woman can attract a man in her sleep because she loves who she is, big or small, tall or short and no one can say otherwise. She can also 'see' herself in a happy, healthy marriage which is a key ingredient in attracting true love.

A DIVA is the confident lady who knows how to make a man work to earn her heart, mind, and eventually her body. She is unpredictable, down-to-earth, and has it going on, in general. She is confident yet humble and sexy yet intriguing. She never looks for a man to take care of her but is not crazy enough to turn down a good man who wants to treat her like a queen. (Note to all of you independent women out there, some of you are taking this independent thing too damn far and messing stuff up for the rest of us. Don't be a fool. If the man wants to open your door and buy you dinner, let him, eat, and say thank you. Woo, finally got that off my chest!)

The DIVA has the 'it' factor oozing from her pores. She may or may not be a model look-a-like. She may or may not be thin, and as a matter of fact, some of the best DIVA s I have ever met were plus size women who always had several men wanting to get at them. The DIVA understands that beauty radiates from the inside out, and she is constantly repeating, "I am a man magnet, and every man in here wants to date me!" This is the girl you will become once you are armed with the knowledge of how to understand men and catch one.

Rule #9: Men Are Hunters by Nature

It is Mother Nature's way of ticking off strong, independent women and keeping the gene pool flowing. As the hunter, the man loves a chase and prides himself on being able to capture the woman not many men can get, and who was not easy for him to catch. Just think about it. Ask any hunter which deer he is most proud of and that hangs on the fireplace mantle. He will tell you that it was not necessarily the largest deer (most attractive woman) but the deer that all the other hunters, including him, tried to catch but was the hardest deer to catch.

The deer that is the hardest to catch is easy to spot because it has what is called the largest rack (antlers). The larger the rack, the older and wiser the deer is. For a woman, a rack would be equivalent to having DIVA self-confidence. Only the hunters with the best skill can catch the older and wiser deer. When these hard to catch deer are finally caught, you would think these men struck gold when you hear them rave about their catch. When I say "catch" this means that he has captured your heart and willingness to give him a chance to earn your hand in marriage.

Men must be able to hunt you, you should not hunt them. They must feel that once they have gotten you, they have a prized possession that the other men could not conquer. The more they work for you, the more they appreciate you once you catch them, and the better they will treat you in the end. Yes, I said you catch them because a man doesn't understand that we actually do the choosing, not them.

Rule #10: Men Need 'Me' Time

Men do not like to feel smothered. Like women, men have their mood swings, and during this time, they need to pull away from you and the relationship. Do not, I repeat, do not freak out on him. You really shouldn't be affected anyway because you will have at least two other guys on the side until you two are 'official'. If you feel the need to vent, call a girlfriend, yell in a pillow, or get out of the house.

Please hear me loud and clear. Do not complain to him that he is not communicating with you, spending time with you or calling three times a day as he had. Give him his space, breathe, and trust that he will come running back with open arms to the DIVA fox you are. Just remember that EVERY dog — not saying your man is a dog, listen to the point — comes back for his bone! Pay attention, though. If he is disappearing on you for weekends at a time, lying, hanging with the boys ALL the time, and not spending any time with you for a period that lasts longer than two weeks, there is a problem, and we will discuss the signs of an inevitable break up in Chapter 14.

Rule #11: Do Not Spend More than 15 Seconds Talking About the Kids

I know that your kids are your world; but try your hardest to not talk about them too much when on dates with your potential love. Yes, I know that you do not get out much, and you are worried if little Timmy will color on your cream leather couch. Everything will be okay. Just have fun and stop worrying about the kids. You left them with a trusty sitter, and they are probably in bed by now, so relax. To be completely honest, he does not care about the kids yet and really does not want to hear about them at this point in the relationship. He may be a great guy, but right now, he simply wants to get to know you as he tries his hardest to get you in bed. You have not hooked him yet to make him want to learn about the kids. So, save the baby-throwing-up-all-over-your-suit stories for the retired neighbor next door.

You are clear that your end goal is to attract a healthy relationship with your perfect partner. You have healed your issues or are at least in the process of ACTIVELY healing your limiting beliefs and residual hurts so that you are open to receive love. You have your list of guidelines on how to be the kind of woman who can attract a good man who is serious about having a long-term relationship and you know exactly what not to do to push away a good man or stay in a relationship with a Don't Wanter. You will date and carry yourself like a woman who expects to attract a husband. Armed with the knowledge that 80% of women are clueless about, you are now graduating from the Ivy League and are ready to successfully date! In the next chapter, I will teach you how to date like a pro and increase your options.

Chapter 8.
Securing Three Dates A Week

By now, you have made a detailed list of your future perfect partner's characteristics. You have trained your mind and body to become the DIVA that you are meant to be. Lastly, you have learned the psychology of a man, and you are now ready to race – I mean date! How are you going to get three dates a week?

Pay special attention. You must follow these steps to a T, and don't go adding your own stuff and messing up the program that you are paying me to teach you.

The Moral Issue

Now let me guess, you are that girl who grew up in the church and whose mother told you that no man wants to marry a whore, slut, or loose woman, so presenting yourself as a good girl at all times is important. This probably means the idea of dating multiple men at a time implies that you would appear to be what your mother warned you not to be. Well let me be clear, I am not telling you to sleep with these men or even to kiss them all. I am just telling you to date and have fun because life is short, and that clock is ticking!

To date means that you are in the process of accepting applications and reviewing resumes. You are not hiring anybody yet for the potential opportunity of being your man. If they have not even been hired yet, it stands to reason that they should not be getting the benefits before it has been determined that they are worthy, deserving, or right for the position. Too many women are giving up the goods while dating a man who has not committed to them yet. I am not advocating casual sex. As a matter of fact, I advise you to wait until you are married, but I know that many women are not going to restrain their sexual appetites, so I have presented some rules on the when, how, and who as it relates to sex.

I repeat, do NOT have sex with or kiss multiple guys at the same time while dating.

Just remember to be honest about your intentions. You are not to lead anyone on and make him believe that you are into him while dating other guys. It does not take more than three to five dates to determine whether you like a guy. If the guy does not express that he is in the market for a committed relationship, keep it moving, period!

The Benefits

Now that we have taken care of the moral question, let's look at some good reasons why dating more than one man at a time works:

It's a numbers game

The more men you meet, the higher your chances of finding the one who is best for you. The more men you date, the better you get at knowing what attracts men as you develop a comfort level and confidence, which is a major turn on for men. The more men you date, the more comfortable you get with setting boundaries. The more men you date, the less likely you will be to settle and tolerate a loser just because you don't want to be home on Saturday nights. The more men you date, the more you will recognize when the warning bells are ringing, and your instincts are telling you to stop, drop, and roll the heck away from a Don't Wanter!

It increases your options

When you date more than one man at a time, you also decrease your chances of wasting time. If it is not working out with someone you have been dating for three weeks, you are free to let him go because you have the other options on the side. Remember, I am not telling you to be a slut puppy. Please do not sleep with three men at a time, and when caught, tell the men I told you to do it! If you keep sex out of the picture, things become less complicated. Now back to my point.

As you are dating several men at a time, you get to pick the best one you can get.

I know plenty of men who hate this advice although they themselves follow it. The men often ask me if I advise a woman to lie about how many men she is seeing, and my answer is "No!" I was always upfront and honest about seeing other people. When I met my ex, I was dating another man, but things were not progressing. No sex or commitment was involved. My ex and I instantly clicked, and I told him upfront that I was seeing someone else casually because I believed that dating and meeting people was very important to single people. He understood and respected me for my honesty and admitted to casually seeing someone as well. We both believed that it would have been unrealistic to believe that the other person had no life and did not entertain other options before meeting each other. When he asked me for a commitment, I told him that I first had to stop dating the other guy and tell him that I was not interested. I was not really feeling the other guy, so everything came together at a perfect time. He admired that I was a) Honest with him about my dating practice and b) Unwilling to deceive someone else by getting into a committed relationship without first ending my association with the other man.

You have now become a laid-back challenge that is not needy.

You now have the power. If he doesn't call, you're alright because you have someone else to occupy your time instead of checking your phone 50 million times a day to see if he has called. If he doesn't want to take you out, this is fine with you because you are busy anyway. He will sense that you are not 'sweating' him, and this will make you a challenge to him. Like a dog chasing a bone, you will keep him working for you until he catches his prize — you!

The men you are dating are doing it too.

Men date without guilt until they are in a committed relationship. They understand that you should never put all of your eggs in one basket. They understand that you must take it slow and not get too emotional too soon. They understand that it will not click with every woman they date, and when things don't work out, they say, "it's time to move on." They understand that dating is not cheating unless a mutual verbal commitment has been established. They understand that dating should be fun, carefree, and that they are not getting married to you tomorrow just because you two are dating today.

The following reasons are NOT the right reasons to date three men at a time:

a) To be emotionally disconnected (because you are afraid of being hurt or disappointed) so that you are not vulnerable enough to fall in love with the right person.
b) To be a player who wants multiple men sweating you and paying for your entertainment.
c) Because you don't have an end goal.

Remember the end game! You will be going on dinner dates, fun outings, and having fun and thought-provoking phone conversations with the opposite sex without having sex, for the purpose of choosing the right person with whom to pursue a long term committed relationship.

The Sources

Online Dating

Online is a great place to start getting out there to meet many types of men.

❤

I offer online dating coaching as part of my one-on-one coaching package to help alleviate the uncertainty and confusion that comes with online dating. With coaching I walk step by step through the process I will share with you here. If you proceed with an open mind and the goal to have fun, you will find online dating enjoyable and rewarding. The goal of online dating is to put out to the Universe that you are ready and open to attracting The One. What usually happens with my clients is that once they are willing to be open to online dating, the right guy shows up offline. Online dating offers excellent dating practice and development of a comfortability with interacting with the opposite sex. Dating with confidence is power!

Sign up on a minimum of three (3) quality online dating sites. Some sites have a better selection of men than others, so please research the right sites for you. There is an art to online dating, so make sure you pay close attention to the following steps.

Step #1: Choose Your Sites

There are many specialized sites available to accommodate just about anyone. For example, many of my beautiful plus size DIVA s do not like the hassle of wondering if the guy will disappear once they meet in person. These women prefer to meet men who prefer plus size women. Plenty of these men exist. If you are heavy set, several online dating sites exist for plus-size women. Just do an Internet search for plus-size online dating sites and several should pop up. Remember not to let your insecurities about your size or any perceived shortcoming stand in the way. You are vivacious, big, and beautiful; and plenty of men out there prefer you over the skinnier women. If you are over 40, try *SingleAndOver40.com*. If you live in farm country, *FarmersOnly.com*, may be the right site for you. This recommendation goes for single mothers, people with disabilities, those affiliated with a particular religion, etc. There are ups and downs with every site I surveyed.

Here are my online dating site picks in no particular order. These sites have more ups than downs in my opinion: *OkCupid.com,*

PlentyofFish.com, *Match.com*, *EliteSingles.com*, and *CoffeeMeetsBagel.com*.

There are online dating sites that I recommend you stay away from if you are searching for a serious long-term relationship. If you are reading this book, that includes you! These online sites are for individuals who are simply looking for hookups. Stay away from these sites. You do not need that kind of drama in your life!

Step #2: Be Safe!

Please keep in mind that you must use caution, instincts, and common sense when using any dating sites. Under no circumstances should you place yourself in harm's way when meeting someone you have communicated with online for the first time.

Do not do the following:

- Do not meet someone from one of these sites and invite them to your home within the first four weeks of meeting them.
- Do not allow your online date to pick you up from your home, job, or any friends' or relatives' homes for the first 5-10 dates.
- Do not take trips or destination vacations with him within the first three months.

Step #3: Your Picture

Get a professional picture taken or find your most flattering photo and post it on the site. Do not post pictures of you with your dog, cat, kids, mother, friends, ex boyfriends, coworkers, etc.! Just post a picture of your beautiful DIVA self. Please be honest and make sure that it is an up-to-date picture.

Step #4: Your Profile

Think long and hard before composing your profile. What do you want to say that will pique the interest of your potential perfect partner? Look at the profile of the other women on the site. Pay extra attention to the ones that stand out, as well as the ones that are boring or a turn off. Try not to write a book. The men will stop reading after the first two paragraphs, so keep it short. Try not to come off as too independent – but do express that you have hobbies you enjoy doing. Try not to come off bitter or angry with harsh warnings rather than compelling messages. For example, don't say: "All players need not apply. I am looking for a relationship, not a booty call, so if you are that type of guy, don't even think about contacting me!" Who would want to meet someone who wrote something like that? Just be a DIVA and allow your divinity, intelligence, and vivacious attitude to be expressed on that page.

Step #5: Let Him Come to You

Even in cyberspace, you have to let him make the first move. I know it sucks, but I did not make the rules. If you make the first move and he doesn't respond, this will be a blow to your ego even though his not responding to you could have nothing to do with your picture or profile. As cute as I am (smile), I have only received one response from the men I have emailed first. The one man who did respond told me that he likes to do the chasing and does not like it when a female chases him, and I never heard from him again. Go figure! I know that some of you have stories to the contrary but if you are still single just remember that we don't make our dating choices based on exceptions to the rule. The chances are high that either you will strike out or choose the wrong one who will reveal that he's not the one for you in the long run.

Step #6: Follow Up

Some of the men who email you will not be Denzel Washington or Matthew McConaughey but give some of them a chance. Think of it as practice. If you cannot see yourself, for whatever reason, going on a date with a particular guy, just send him a reply telling him that you are dating another match or are taking a break from dating right now. This is just common courtesy.

Step #7: Communicate via email First

Let him email you back and forth at least 2 to 4 times before you give him your phone number. It is weird how this happens, but many times you may start communicating with a match, and he will just disappear. It's life; just move on to the other 10 matches you have in your box and leave him alone. If you give him your phone number and he calls you, talk maybe 2 to 3 times and then meet with him if he asks. You do not want to email or talk on the phone with him for too long. You are not looking for a pen pal; you are looking for a perfect partner. If he gives you the creeps over the phone, then do not meet him, and do not answer his calls. Always follow your instincts!

Step #8 The First Meeting

The first meeting should only be about 20 minutes long. Suggest the bookstore, the coffee shop, or the park during daytime hours. It must be a place that is well lit and have lots of people around. Make sure that you drive your own car. This will eliminate you being stuck with someone you do not gel with or who, worse, gets on your darn nerves.

This rule should also apply for those coming in from out of town to meet you. Remember, he should always be the one who is coming to meet you from out of town for the first date or meeting. However, he should not be coming to see just you. He should have personal, family, or business options with which he can or will engage himself while in town. Never have an out of town online date spend the night at your home during his first few visits. I do not care how close you believe you two are after months of phone conversations. Give yourself an exit strategy just in case you have no connection or chemistry. You should always let him know upfront that this will only be a simple lunch meeting. Therefore, if the date is not going well, you will not be stuck with someone all day just because he came from out of town.

I made the mistake of going to dinner with a guy on the first meeting. He talked about his muscles, the gym, and how fine he was for nearly an hour and a half. I wanted to throw up in my mouth and run but did not want to be rude. The point is to keep the first meeting short, sweet and cheap.

Speed Dating

Speed dating is so much fun! You get to meet several men in one night and see which ones you want to see again. The place is well lit, you are sober, and you have an excuse to leave or end the date if you are not feeling him because the bell will ring when your time together is up! Make sure you come prepared and with a set of questions in your head. Some women come with a list of formal questions as if they are interviewing the men. This is not a good idea because you never want to create an impersonal atmosphere. Have your list in your head and write your notes down after the speed dating session. Make sure the questions just flow naturally so he has no clue you have a list of questions in your purse. The list of questions is great because if he answers any questions incorrectly, you can scratch him off the list. My only advice is to be open and on your best real behavior. Do not try too hard and do not participate with a poor attitude. Just have fun!

Blind Dates

Understand that arranged marriages are nothing new and are often very successful in other cultures. Still, most people dread blind dates, but they can be very rewarding. Your friends and family usually know you better than you think, and sometimes they know a friend of a friend who will complement your personality. Sometimes they get it right. Sometimes they don't, but you will never know if you don't try.

A woman often chooses a mate based on where she is at the time she is looking for love instead of choosing someone based on where she is going. We are often evolving and being shaped by our life experiences. What we desire today, we may not desire tomorrow. If you have recently left an abusive relationship, sit down and take time to heal. No matter how ready you think you are, you are not yet ready five months to a year later. Get counseling or coaching to assist you in forgiving, healing and moving on. Do not make the mistake of looking for someone to help you heal. Many abused women jump from one abusive relationship to another because they have not taken the time to heal or they choose an extremely nice man with whom they are incompatible only because they feel safe with him. After some time, these women wake up from the fog of low self-esteem and realize that they have chosen the wrong man because they choose a guy based on where they were, which was hurt, broken, and abused. They did not give themselves time to heal and choose the right mate who could meet their needs for who they were becoming.

Your family and close friends are often aware of who you are even if you have forgotten. They are also aware of your potential and goals, so they can tell if a man is the right man for you. I am not saying to choose solely based on your parents, friends, and family's opinion. I am simply saying that they are a great source of determining if a person has your best interest at heart.

Jazz Clubs, Parks, Bookstores, Coffee Shops

These are nice venues to meet mature, professional, established men. Keep in mind that you are going for quality. Higher quality places usually attract higher quality people. These are not the places to bring your entourage. You are not a rock star. Keep it light and roll with one or two girlfriends, but any more than that will scare a man from approaching you.

When you spot someone who interests you, make sure to determine his interest by giving him the eye test. The eye test is when you look at the guy and hold a stare just long enough to let him know that you are interested and not so long that he thinks that you are a stalker. If he looks away, just assume he is gay — it's better for your ego. If he returns your gaze, make sure you smile and touch your hair, or lick your lips subtly, or turn your body slightly toward him. These are all mating signs that say, "Hey cutie, come talk to me."

Sports Bar

A sports bar is a man's playground. He will probably pay more attention to the game than the fact that a DIVA is in the room, but during the commercials, he will get a chance to notice that a woman is enjoying the game as much as he is. This is a great place to frequent especially if you are a sports fan.

Special note: You are a DIVA, and a DIVA understands that a way to a man's heart is through his mind, stomach, lower extremities, and sports. I know most of us ladies could care less about sports, but if you really want to stand out from the crowd, be sexy, smart, a challenge, and love sports. Woman like this are so rare that when found, men hold onto them for dear life. Just remember you are a lady, not one of the boys, so no cursing, spitting, being loud, slapping the guy next to you on the back, or getting drunk.

The Gym

Going to the gym is like going to the candy store; sexy men are everywhere. You know these men care about their appearance, and you will be wearing your sexy gear and turning heads left and right. The only downfall is that men are gun shy at the gym. Leery, half-naked women at the gym have shot them down so many times that they'd rather err on the side of caution and just look.

This is the only place that you can make the first move. You must be subtle about it, though. Try not to spend too much time in the cardio section. Work out where the men are, which is the free weight section. You can ask the cutie next to you how to use a machine of interest or to spot you on your bench press. Make sure that you are pleasant and laid back and not overly flirtatious. It is worth mentioning that you are there to workout, get fit, and improve your health, too. That said, you should not wear a ton of makeup, high heels, and your hair looking like you just stepped out of the salon. A DIVA never looks like she is looking for a man. On the other hand, please do not go to the gym wearing a headscarf, head wrap, do-rag, or any other unsightly headgear. Have you ever noticed when women take off these head garments their hair is wet anyway? Again, this is so unattractive, as well as ineffective in protecting one's hair from sweat, so please leave them at home. Also, please leave the cell phone in the car or a locker unless you are using it simply for listening purposes. Nothing is worse than a loud woman talking on the phone as she obstructs a weight machine while pretending that she is working out.

Church

Praise the Lord for all the attractive men in the house! I know, we are there to worship, but what is wrong with allowing the good Lord to help us increase our dating options by being open to a spiritual single man. Not all men in church are holy, so be careful. Many Players, Pimps, and Mama's Boys go to church, too! Join the singles ministry at church and get to know the singles at your church who are also looking for love.

Professional Organizations

This is probably one of the best sources of good men. These men are usually ambitious, committed to their goals, professional, and intelligent. These men seem to have their heads on straight more times than not, are more mature in their approach, and understand how to treat a lady. The fact that you are members of the same organization demonstrates that you both have something significant in common. The men I have met from common professional organizations have always been mature, established gentlemen. I am not saying that this will always be the case, but many women have had great experiences with these men, including relationships that have led to successful marriages.

NOT Spots

Notice that I did not mention the local bars, clubs, or weekend hangout spots. The only exception is a sports bar, and I have already explained to you why this is a great way to meet men. The reason why, my foxy DIVA, you will not be looking for a man in the bars, clubs, or local hangout spots is that the type of men who frequent these spots are most likely not the type of men you want to spend your life with or bring around your children. Go to these places for fun and to dance but not to find a man. If you happen to meet one during a night out with the girls, proceed with an open but cautious mind. He may be there simply enjoying a guys' night out. Just don't go to the club looking for your future husband. The guys there are usually chronic partiers trying to talk to as many women as they can. If you enter a relationship with these men and find out that they like to hang with the boys or go out too much, don't be angry or surprised because that's how you met him. My momma used to always say, "The way you start is the way you will finish, so start right!"

In addition, do not, I repeat, do not pay an agency or dating service thousands of dollars to help you find quality men. They sell the hype that when you pay for a service to match you that you get high-quality men who can "afford" this type of service. I find these services to be a waste of time and money, and unfortunately, they do not have a high success rate with all races of women.

If you follow everything that I teach you within this book, you will not have to pay to be matched with anyone. You are learning how to catch your own fish and do so with wisdom. Follow the rules and date with wisdom and you will be on your way to attracting your future love in no time.

Chapter 9.
The Dating Process

As I previously stated, there are rules to dating. The dating rules for single women are different for single women with children. This process separates the girls from the DIVAs. This is also the area where many women sabotage their potential success with a man. Most women have no idea what they naturally do to turn off men. Most women operate from their feelings and think a man will appreciate and relate to a woman's feelings in the same manner.

If you want to get a head start on finding your perfect partner or you are tired of striking out when it comes to the dating game, pay attention to the following rules and do not make up your own exceptions. After your eyes have been opened to what I am about to share with you, you will see which behaviors have been getting in your way and why some women seem to have more men falling over them than they care to admit.

Dating Rules for Mothers

(Single women, there is a wealth of information that you can learn here. Keep reading!)

Here are some rules especially for single women with children to use while dating:

Rule #1: Your children come first

No matter how long it has been since the last time you have been held by a man, been taken out by a man, or made love to by a man, your kids are your utmost priority. No man will respect you or your children if you do not make this clear from the beginning. If your child gets sick on a date night, reschedule. If he doesn't like kids, kick his butt to the curb.

Rule #2: Don't date expecting to meet your husband or a father for your child.

We are all guilty of it. We want love so bad that we cross our fingers and hold our breath hoping we will finally meet The One today. If you expect and know that soon enough you will meet your One, you won't place so much expectation on the date itself. You cannot enjoy someone on a date if you have too many expectations before he has even entered the door. You cannot be successful in dating if you don't show up. Just because I had you plan your wedding day earlier doesn't mean that you should walk around with a magnify glass wondering on each date if this person is The One! The exercise I had you do was for the purposes of seeing yourself getting married and creating the powerful magnifying energy of 'expectation'. If you can see yourself in a relationship being loved in a healthy way and getting married, it can and will happen. If you show up to each date without stress and worry because you know that even if this one isn't The One, The One will eventually show up, your husband will show up. I guarantee this! To *know* that you know beyond a shadow of a doubt is the key ingredient that draws what you want to you faster. I call it quiet assurance or the power of attraction.

With that said, you cannot show up in the present if you are already in the future, as you fantasize about what he will look like in a white tux on your wedding day. Enjoy your date, leave all expectations at the door, and you will find that your chances of securing another date increase that much more.

Rule #3: Hold off introducing the kids to your new love until you know you are heading to marriage with this man.

Ok, let me clarify myself for all my confused mothers out there who feel that simply dating him for two months and thinking that you are in love is enough reason to bring him around the kids, have him pick them up from school and stay in the house alone with them while you are at work. Make sure you have done a background check, he has proposed to you, and you two are in the process of planning the wedding before you start bringing him around the kids on a regular basis. I know I am getting a lot of frowns and eye rolling on this one, but think about it, if your children get attached to yet another man and things do not work out, it will send the wrong message to your children and will cause them to experience loss once again. Not to mention that sometimes, we misjudge people while we are wearing the rose-colored glasses during the early stage, and the man you think is Prince Charming, may be a pervert.

Now, let me clarify, I am NOT saying to never let your man meet your kids before the wedding, I am saying don't let him hang out with them on a regular basis until you have a serious commitment, such as marriage. Your man should meet your children within the first three months of dating so that you are able to see how he interacts with them. He definitely should meet them before you give him your 'goods'. However, make sure that he is not meeting them as "Mommy's boyfriend."

After a few months of dating, set up a meeting to see how he interacts with the kids. Introduce him as a friend and go for ice cream or to the park. If the kids get a good vibe, you can then move forward with the relationship. However, if your children do not feel comfortable around him, or if he acts as if he doesn't even care to make an effort, reconsider him as a potential life partner. Children, especially the younger ones, often see the true nature of someone, and I value what children feel about a person because their feelings are usually unfiltered. Remember not to force the development of a relationship between the kids and your man. The children may still have hang-ups about you and their dad not being together. Give it time and make sure that he is who he says he is, and please follow the next rule!

Rule #4: Do a background check on the man before you get too serious about him.

You have enough to worry about without worrying about someone stealing your stuff or harming your kids. You will probably never be in this position because you always follow your instincts, but sometimes we overlook a few things. You can easily go online and pay a company about $50 for a background check. Felony criminal history records can be obtained from most local sheriffs or police departments. You can also do a free online search in most county and state sex offender records. For instance, in Georgia, these records can be accessed on the Georgia Bureau of Investigations website.

You are not looking for something to be wrong with him; you just want to use wisdom and ensure that everything is right. Other sites rely on personal testimonies or better yet, horror stories, to provide personal background information. One such site is *www.dontdatehimgirl.com*. I will get into further depth about this in the next chapter.

Rule #5: No sex in the house while kids are home

I do not want to get too philosophical here, but your bed should be sacred and only shared with your perfect partner. You should wait until you know he loves you and commits to being part of you and your child's life before even considering sex, but if you feel the need to get your 'fix', let him take you to a nice hotel or to his house. In the Native American tradition, it is believed that a person's spirit remains in the bed they have slept in until the bed is burned. Do you really want to have to burn a mattress every time a relationship ends? In addition, kids see and hear all, and you do not want them to walk in and see mommy talking to Mr. Man's little man. If you MUST have sex in the house, at least make sure that it is late at night, the door to your room is locked, and the kids are in a deep sleep. (No, do not give them Robitussin.) Please make sure the music is playing and you are not screaming loud enough to wake up the kids!

Rule #6: Never ever let your kids overhear or see you arguing with a man.

Children do not understand that fighting is normal and that adults fight sometimes. All they know is that their mother is upset because of some man. This can affect the way they view your new love because in their minds, all they know is that he is mean or bad because he made mommy cry.

Rule #7: Do not have your children refer to him as "Uncle" anything.

It always amazes me when I hear children calling their mother's boyfriends or stepfathers "Uncle." I do not think you want your child to believe that it's okay to kiss their brother or date a cousin. This is confusing to a child, and a little mind can take this the wrong way. Introduce him as Mr. So and So until you two are married, then let the child decide to call him something more affectionate if the father is not in the child's life.

Rule #8: Listen to your instincts at all times.

As you can tell, this is a big one for me. Your inner voice is there to protect you. You will never go wrong if you listen to it and follow its warning.

Setting Up Dates

Whatever your status Is, as a single woman with or without children, you should be asked out by the Wednesday before the weekend.

You should drive your own car and meet him at the location until after the fourth date or whenever you feel comfortable having him pick you up from your home.

If he asks you out – and he should be the one asking you out – he should pay. Keep your hands out of your purse when the bill comes. You can test him before the date by finding out his reaction to a (made up) conversation you say you had with, say, your brother. In this scenario, your brother was complaining about a girl he took out on a date who tried to pay for her own meal when he was the one who asked her out. Listen to how your guy responds. The way he responds will determine if he will even get a date with you.

The First Date

Mastering the first date is no easy task, and it is sometimes the main reason potentially great relationships do not materialize afterward. Many women find dating to be a scary, daunting task because they do not know what to say or how to act on the first date to ensure the man is so captivated by them that he continues to ask them out again until an eventual commitment is formed. Fret no more. I will give you the secrets that will make some women dating champs while other women who don't know the secrets will remain dating tragedies. You will learn how to date like a rock star and fall in love with the art of dating. Follow these suggestions, and I guarantee if you are interested in him, he will ask you out a second, third and fourth time.

Rule #1: Dress classy and look smashing.

Shave your legs and underarms. Do not chew gum or smoke. If you are going to wear perfume, wear a small amount. Please wear a dress, do your hair and put on a little makeup. Men are visual and love women in dresses who care about their appearances. A dress makes you look soft, feminine, and shows off your legs. Makeup lets him know that you did not come to play and that you love yourself enough to amplify your beautiful features. No shortcuts ladies!

If you can't tell by now, the way you dress for a date is a big deal. It is a big deal because it is your first impression before you even open your mouth. The way you dress also affects the way you feel on the date. There is a different feeling when you wear revealing clothes verses classy and sexy clothes. Less clothes triggers a mating signal in the subconscious male mind. This is evolutionary and occurs subconsciously – and will not change no matter how many "Slut Walks" Amber Rose organizes. Less is more. That is, the less you reveal is more of a turn on you will be for him! Do not reveal all the secrets God has given you, some things should be left to the imagination. It has been proven that women wear fewer clothes during ovulation to increase the chances of mating, so a woman who dresses as if she is looking to mate usually attracts the man who only wants to mate – get my drift? Do keep the body covered but try not to dress like a nun. Find a style that incorporates a lot of class, a dash of sexy, and a little edge.

Rule #2: Smile, Smile, Smile!

A study was done to determine men's selection patterns for beauty. The study asked men to rate which women they thought were more beautiful by looking at various photos. They showed each man two pictures, one picture was of a woman smiling and the other was of a woman who was not smiling. Many of the women who were not smiling fit the stereotype of beautiful, model-like women, but most of the men chose the women who were smiling, no matter how tall, thin, or attractive she appeared. Here is a powerful secret: Men are attracted to feminine women. Women who wear smiles as part of their daily wardrobe are perceived to be very feminine, approachable and attractive.

Rule #3: Let him plan the date and start the conversation.

I know your Girl-Power nature is flinching on this one, but a man's greatest joy is being able to please the object of his affection. It also allows you to see his true interest in you, based on how much effort he puts into planning the date. In addition, letting him be the one to initiate the conversation sends a signal to him that you trust, respect, and accept him as the man. This will make a great impression on him and can be a great start to a potentially wonderful future!

Rule #4: Be interested and ask questions about him without coming off as if you are interviewing him.

Use questions to get to know him; and keep them light and on topics that make you both laugh. Leave the serious questions for the fourth date or beyond. You want him laughing and feeling good as much as possible. This way, he will associate feeling good and smiling with your beautiful face. Here are some suggested questions to ask:

- What are his hobbies?
- What was the first car he ever bought?
- Does he enjoy his profession? If not, move on quickly.
- What was his funniest or most embarrassing moment ever?
- What was the town like where he grew up?
- Who is his favorite comedian?
- How does he get along with his mother?

Rule #5: Do not ask the wrong questions.

Here are some example no-no questions and none of your business...yet:

- How well do he and his ex-wife or child's mother get along?
- Does he pay child support?
- What is his credit score, salary, and financial portfolio?
- Any questions concerning death or sad subjects.
- Any questions about his spiritual, political, pro-life or pro-choice beliefs, or his feelings about homosexuals.

Rule #6: Do not drink until the second date.

If you must drink, have just one glass and whatever you do, do not get drunk. A drunken date is a bad date and a DIVA does not mix sexy with being a drunk.

❤

Rule #7: Pay attention to how he treats the waiter.

If he treats the waiter like crap, this is not a good sign. The way he treats the people who serve him is a great indication as to the way he will treat you. Not to mention, on 20/20, they did a story about how waiters would spit in the food, put ashes in the food and God knows what else to the customers who were rude to them.

Rule #8: Have fun and laugh at his jokes.

All men want to feel that they are making a good impression on a woman. When you laugh at his jokes, this gives his ego a huge boost. It also forms a connection between you, so keep the smiles and laughter coming.

Rule #9: Please refrain from talking about any of these things.

Avoid talking about your money, his money, credit, your baby-daddy, exes, his plans for marriage, kids, puppies, sappy women's movies, Oprah, astrology, your weight issues, your insecurities, or the fact that you read this book. All of these topics are mood killers and way too heavy for the first date. Memorize this list and keep your lips shut on several of these topics until a committed relationship is formed. Please note that some of these topics should remain buried and in the past.

Rule #10: No kissing or talking about sex on the first date.

Be flirtatious and intriguing but not sluttish. You should not be talking about anything concerning sex with your date. Your mouth should not touch his at all on the first date. Do I really need to explain why one-night stands don't work? I get questions from fellow DIVAs all the time who ask me what they should do if they really like a guy who they have slept with too soon. My answer is to leave him alone and start over with someone new, and this time, learn from your mistake. Ok, I know that this is not what you want to hear, so let me say this: it can work. I have seen many people marry a first date sexual encounter. Out of the ten that I can think of, only three are still married. Out of the three still married, only one of them has a peaceful, loving, drama-free marriage. The odds are stacked against you when you move too fast in a relationship. No one wants anything if it is too easy or cheap, and if you easily give it up on the first date, you are now a booty call or throw back. One of the worst feelings is knowing you have been used for sex, so don't do it. I do not care how great the connection, chemistry, or conversation is. Keep your legs closed on the first, second, and tenth date. That means just wait and let him grow to learn and love you first before he gets the goods.

Rule #11: Enjoy and be yourself.

A man or anyone, for that matter, can tell when someone is trying 'too hard' to make a good impression. Sometimes this trying too hard can send the signal that you are fake or phony and are not to be trusted. Being confident in yourself and knowing he is the lucky one who is able to take you out is a must for making a great first impression. Remember: all you have to do is sit back, smile a lot, and let the fish (man and his efforts) come to you!

Making Him Fall Hard for You: The Art of Seduction

Scientists have figured out that a chemical is released in our brain whenever we begin to feel the sensations of love for another person. This chemical is called phenylethylamine, or PEA for short. This reaction can be intentionally ignited in your object of attraction. When you combine the following gestures or behaviors, you will send jolts of that love chemical, PEA, into your date.

Extend your gaze.

If you have not watched the movie *Memoirs of a Geisha*, please do. It is an excellent movie, but more importantly for you, there is a point when the main character is training to become a Geisha, and she is learning the art of stopping a man in his tracks with a simple gaze. When she finally learns this art, she is able to make a man riding on a bike run into a food stand and fall over. Now that is power, and that is the skill you must develop, my DIVA-in-training. When you have the power to stop a man in his tracks with your gaze and/or walk, you are on your way to having men eating out of your hands. Look him deep in the eyes with a slight smile for an extended period until he looks away. While gazing for less than three seconds, think to yourself, "You will fall for me and fall hard you must!" Feel the power fill your entire body. When you give him an extended gaze, and he seems swept away, subtly look down at his lips. If he is gazing back and you two are in conversation, he will feel that PEA rush, as long as you don't break the gaze and continue to maintain your level of confidence. When you gaze at someone with confidence in your eyes without looking away and a physical attraction exists between you, the falling in love hormone rushes through your veins and increases the chances of a love connection.

Compliment him.

Men love compliments. You can overdo it, however, because you may swell his head and appear as if you are sweating him, which is not DIVA-ish at all. Simply point out little things you notice about him in casual conversation or listen to what he talks about the most and what he is passionate about, and compliment him on his drive, great talent, or ambition. Try to stay away from compliments on his appearance. You do not want to appear shallow. If he is attractive, he has heard it all from the other Desperados trying to impress him. You are different from all the other women, and you look beyond the physical.

Tell him stories that keep him wanting more.

Don't tell him your life story but do keep him intrigued by giving him something to ponder after he leaves you. This takes a bit of skill, chemistry, and having some great, interesting stories. If you are a reader, this task becomes easier because you can enlighten and intrigue men with the vastness of your understanding. For example, you can share something uncontroversial but deep you read in an article or self-help book that intrigued you and made a lasting impression on your life. These stories should only be shared with someone with whom you have great connection or chemistry. Test the stories with your honest girlfriend and ask her if it held her interest. Maybe it is something that happened on the job, when you went to the grocery store or maybe something you heard on the news. Try not to be too chatty and be aware of his body language to recognize whether he is bored with the story. Try to keep the tales upbeat and positive. You do not want to come off as a gossip columnist or a pessimist.

Dilate your pupils.

Another study was conducted comparing two photos of the same person side by side. When asked which photo was more attractive, the photo in which the person's pupils were dilated was selected 9 out of 10 times. This is the reason why all Disney characters have dilated pupils. Looking into dilated pupils initiates the PEA response and causes the person looking at you to feel a strong sense of attraction. Do not go out to the eye doctor and get drops to put in your pupils so that they appear larger. Simply think about and feel the moments in which you experienced love or euphoric feelings, and this will cause your pupils to dilate.

Mimic or 'mirror' his words, body language, and gestures.

This is the first law of how to win over people. People love to see themselves in someone else. I dated this guy I was greatly intrigued by and attracted to, and we grew to really care about each other. I could not, for the life of me, figure out why our attraction for each other was so strong. Then one day it hit me when we were in conversation. I used a word specific to my industry, and later in the conversation, he used that exact same word. It was amazing because although I noticed that he had mimicked me, I actually really liked hearing him repeat that word. He also had a talent for mirroring me when we were together. If I sat a certain way, he sat that way, too. I felt as though we had so much in common, and he felt the same about me. This was because we both were naturally mirroring and mimicking each other.

When you are in sync with someone, you will naturally start to mimic or mirror some of their gestures and words. If he says that it was a "beautiful" day today, and he loves days when the "sun is shining so brightly," you can repeat those words during the conversation. For example, when you talk about your trip to Florida, you may say that you really enjoyed your vacation because every day was a "beautiful" day, and you really enjoyed lying out on the beach because the "sun was shining so brightly." Whatever the words or the topic, just pay attention. When he folds his hands, fold yours. When he talks with his hands, you can make some of the same gestures.

With practice, he won't even notice and will come to enjoy it subconsciously. You can even practice with the guys you don't care to have long-term relationships with but would like to keep as friends. After a while, these men will come to really like you and not even know why. This is why you see women who may not be runway models but have the best-looking guys with them. They make men feel good about themselves by mirroring their words, behaviors, and body language.

Touch his hands when he makes you laugh - but only after he has started to flirt with you.

Physical contact is the most effective tool to demonstrate interest in the other person. It only works if there is an attraction between you both. There must be chemistry and he must show you that he is attracted to you first or you will come off as desperate and easy. A DIVA never wants to come off as desperate or easy, so pay attention to the signs he shows you. When you touch his hand or knee while sharing a comical moment, it sends the message that you are interested. This can only strengthen the connection if there is chemistry between the both of you.

Don't get caught up in his words.

Men understand that women love to hear sweet nothings. Stay focused and appear to be amused and doubtful at the same time. I know it sounds a bit confusing and this will take practice but interacting with a man is like fishing. Sometimes you have to throw a line out there and then reel it in. When he tells you that you are the most beautiful creature he has ever seen, say, "Well, I am sure you tell all of the other creatures that you meet the same thing, but it's nice to hear, so thank you!"

Don't talk too much or reveal too much about yourself.

Don't start off with your dark secrets! The fact that you suffered a nervous breakdown when your husband of eight years left you, or that you are seeing a therapist because your last boyfriend left you for your best friend is something that should be kept to yourself. Spend more time listening than talking but pay attention to whether he is interested in learning more about you.

Flirt, Flirt, Flirt.

Flirt, but not too much; there is a fine line. You don't want to be perceived as a tease; this can backfire after it pisses off the man. Flirting is an art that starts with the eyes, continues with the smile and culminates with subtle hand gestures in which you touch yourself (hair, arm, etc.). Again, practice with the men you meet along the way that you have no long-term interest in.

Chapter 10.
Do Your Due Diligence

God did not give us a spirit of fear. Moving through the dating world afraid of running into a boogie man at every turn will only attract to you that which you fear. Follow the advice that I give you in this book. Listen to the meditations. Stay on your path. If you still need guidance, call me and get coaching. Pray and know that God created you to experience life more abundantly and this includes being loved in a healthy relationship. This is true even though you may have had many painful experiences in your life. You must believe this before you can attract a healthy relationship.

I have written this section so that you have the wisdom to date safely because the truth is that there are some dishonest people with bad intentions in the world. It is unrealistic to believe that as you are out dating, you won't run into some individuals who can possibly hurt you. Just like when you learn to drive, a good teacher will instruct you on defensive driving so that you are trained to avoid the consequences of careless, poorly trained drivers. We all know that bad drivers exist. Everyone has been cut off by one or more of these jerks who are inconsiderate of the safety of others. This doesn't stop you from getting in your car daily and taking the risk of experiencing an accident so that you are able to reach your destination. The risks are worth the final destination of true love, a life partner, maybe a family, and the amazing memories you will create as a result of this love coming into your life.

Avoid Getting Played

There are so many reasons why women get played, but the number one way to avoid being deceived is to do your own due diligence by confirming that a man is who he says he is, before getting serious or having sex with him. You must do the following when you see that the relationship is moving toward a more serious level. Refer to the information I gave you in the last chapter for more information on carrying out these tasks.

Rule #1: Verify that he is not on the sex offender list. (Before 1st Date)

Sex offender lists are available online and vary from state to state. If you do find something, keep in mind that the court records that landed someone onto the list are public, and you can access them if you need more information.

Rule #2: Google him. (After 2nd date)

You can learn a lot about someone by running a google search and 'stalking' them online. Check out their social media profiles, see if their name comes up in any context that makes you want more information. Follow your instincts.

Rule #3: Run criminal and civil background checks on him. (After 3rd date)

You can also research information in government public records, which include databases for court, criminal, birth, real estate, marriage/divorce, and death. Keep in mind that laws and regulations differ from state to state, so some of these public records are simple enough to access freely online, such as property records, while others will require an administrative fee or be restricted altogether. Rather than researching to find this information on your own, you can use online public records information providers. These services usually charge a fee, but they may be worth it in avoiding deception. Criminal records will reveal information about any arrests and felony convictions, but also about any misdemeanor offences, which can include domestic violence and reckless driving. Civil records will tell you about any legal suits or financial filings either by him or against him, which may tell you a lot about his morality and financial situation and will also record if he has been divorced and whether or not he is paying his child support.

Rule #4: Ask to see physical proof of his STD status before having sex with him. (After 3 months or before you have sex with him)

You should both get STD tests before engaging in sex with a new partner. Some STDs take weeks or months to appear, and either of you may be unaware that you are carrying a sexually transmitted disease.

Rule #5: If it comes up that he was married in the past, ask - no demand - to see a physical copy of the divorce decree. (After 4th date moving into exclusive dating)

Show me the paper! No excuses. For the many reasons I have outlined in this book from emotional and moral to legal and financial risks, you do not want to be involved with a married man.

Rule #6: Meet his family and friends before having sex with him - even if they are all out of town. (Before becoming exclusive)

First, if he doesn't want you to meet his family, it may be because he is telling you lies about who he is or what his situation or past may be. It may be simply because he doesn't get along with his family, but that brings problems also. If you marry a man, or even are seriously committed, you will be committed to his family as well. These people will be your children's family and will be contributing half of their DNA. If they are all crazy, or mean, or have some congenital condition, you may want to reconsider if you want to become part of their family.

Over the years, I have met so many women, including myself, who have been taken through the ringer for closing their eyes and failing to protect themselves by completing this due diligence process of finding out everything they can about the man you are dating exclusively. Many of you may think that what I suggest is being a little excessive and overboard, but when you hear what happened in the following stories, you will realize that I am right.

Wisdom and Age

Age is just a number when it comes to acquiring dating intelligence and understanding men. With the divorce rate reaching over 60 percent, many women are finding themselves in a dating atmosphere that is totally different from that of their ancestors. As more women over 50 become single, they find that the dating game has changed radically since they were last single. This has, unfortunately, led to a spike in the HIV infection rate of women over the age of 50. According to the Centers for Disease Control and Prevention (CDC), AIDS cases among individuals over the age of 50 have increased 22 percent since 1991.

I discovered firsthand that just because a woman is older, she is not immune to heartbreak. While waiting as a witness in criminal court, I heard the case of an educated, slightly overweight, middle-aged, African American woman, who I will refer to as Gloria. She was attempting to have a 60-year-old Caucasian woman with a head-full of long, gray hair, who I will refer to as Vicky, prosecuted for stalking and harassment.

Vicky, a widow for 17 years after 35 years of marriage, met a man who conned her out of her money and trust. He was the first committed relationship she had since the death of her husband. Vicky was excited about the new relationship with a man she hardly knew and looked forward to the potential it had. She testified that for years she had given up on love and didn't believe that at her age she could find it. Then Jeremy, a middle-aged man, showed up in her life, telling her everything she wanted to hear while taking advantage of her loneliness. What she didn't know was that Jeremy was also dating Gloria, as well as five other women.

Once Vicky found out about Gloria, she sent several emails, text messages, and calls to Gloria attached with evidence that Jeremy was dating them both. Vicky even emailed Gloria a picture of her hand on Jeremy's man part to prove that she and Jeremy had been intimate. Gloria responded by pressing charges to get Vicky locked up for harassment after Gloria said her daughter pulled up the illicit picture sent via email.

When Vicky got on the stand to give her side of the story, she broke down in tears and confessed that she knew what she did was wrong, and that she should not have handled the situation in that way. She said she was just hurt and confused after finding out the man she loved was a con artist who used her. She explained how she almost lost her house, retirement savings, and sanity because she trusted and loved Jeremy. She said that she did not contact Gloria to hurt or harass her, but simply wanted to warn her so he didn't use and hurt Gloria the way he did her. The entire courtroom was in tears as the woman poured her heart out and apologized to Gloria for the pain she caused. We all even clapped when they hugged and went on their way.

This entire situation is a great example of what I refer to in my books when I encourage women to do their homework on the person they are dating before giving their heart, mind, body, and money to someone they hardly know. I am confident that neither of the women did their homework by running a full background check, asking for documented proof of his STD status, and getting a physical copy of his divorce certificate. In the section below titled "How I Unknowingly Married A Married Man," I go in depth about my own mistake of failing to complete one step in this discovery process and the price I had to pay because of it. The discovery process is a fact-finding exercise every woman should perform on the man she is seriously dating. A woman should never rely only on her experience or age to determine who to trust with her heart. This process and *all* the steps are important. Every woman should understand the risk she may encounter if any step in this process is overlooked.

Sleeping with the Enemy

Imagine meeting a man who has all the amazing qualities you've been looking for, falling in love, and then moving in with him. After having two children with him, you ask him when he is going to ask for your hand in marriage. He gives you a song and dance about how it will happen soon enough but just not yet. He continues to put off his proposal and you go on accepting his excuses only to find yourself eight years later still playing house with him. You don't really understand why he won't marry you, but you stay because your love and hope keep you there.

It is hard to imagine seeing your man's face every day for eight years and finding out that he was pretty much a stranger to you who had a whole other life that you never knew about. Envision one day you get a call that your man has died in a car accident. All your hopes and dreams for the future are destroyed, and you are left devastated. You can't imagine feeling any worse, but then you stumble upon information about him you never knew. The death of a relative seems to bring everyone out, from those paying their respects to those looking for anything of material value that the dead may have left. Imagine that while dealing with the death of the man you love, you discover that he has children you never knew he had! He has five different children from three different mothers. He was still married to one of these women. Everything that he owns, his insurance policy and the property he purchased in his name, that you and your kids reside in, ALL go to his wife!

You really do believe that you know someone after nearly a decade, and some people are convinced of this after only a couple of months. Love can make a person do crazy things, including compromising their own safety, sanity, and even their lives because we let our hearts rule and tune out what our heads and loved ones are telling us. I am not being paranoid or old fashioned when I stress the importance of inspecting a man's history before things get too serious and not living with someone before marriage. This woman could have been any one of us who lost precious years while waiting on a man who did not deserve our heart. She will now have to lose more time trying to heal and move on from this lesson and she most likely will have trouble loving and trusting again. She spent eight years sleeping with the enemy, so to speak, and the most painful truth is that she allowed it. This is the true story of one of my past clients. Learn from her mistake and never allow someone to just tell you who they are or force you to compromise what you truly want.

How I Unknowingly Married A Married Man

In today's world, a dating single woman with kids can fall victim to so many potential land-mines. Many women have made so many mistakes and suffered so many heartbreaks that they have given up on love. Love, to many women, feels too good to give up on but too painful to keep failing at. Scratch that! Let's be clear: True love is not deceitful or painful. True love does not hurt. The goal of this book is to help you attract true love. I suggest that you never give up, but make sure to arm yourself with enough information so you can avoid the landmines that await today's single woman.

One of the most heart-wrenching dating dangers that a woman can experience is to fall in love with a married man. In Chapter 6, I wrote an entire chapter on how to never date a married man and the pitfalls that a woman could face if she finds herself in this position. I understand that many of you will read this book, say that it was wonderful and walk away never doing what I have suggested or taught you with in this book. With this in mind, I am writing even more about what happened to me when I failed to complete the due diligence process and ended up thinking I was marrying my soulmate, when I was really marrying a monster who happened to still be married. I already know what you are thinking: "What? Did I read the last paragraph correctly? Did Shay really say that she married a married man when she teaches us to avoid a married man like the plague?"

Yes, you read it correctly! I unknowingly married a married man, and I am sharing this painful experience with you so that you will never find yourself in the same situation.

When I met JM, it was what I would describe as serendipitous at first. We met on an online dating site and connected instantly. I met him the day my membership was to expire two hours later. The first time we met in person, it was instant attraction, and everything moved quickly from there.

At the time I was facing unemployment, a foreclosure and severe financial trouble. I had pulled my entire $100,000 savings and invested in an apartment complex redevelopment project that went down the drain when the real estate market crashed in 2007. During the real estate heyday, I knew almost everything there was to know about real estate investment and made a ton of money. I studied and saved, and I eventually worked my way up from residential to commercial investment. It had always been my goal to be a real estate tycoon. I dreamed of owning apartment buildings, condo developments and tall office buildings. I worked for months to secure the perfect project that would benefit my family for a lifetime, as I began to focus on building my empire. Many banks wouldn't consider doing a deal with a woman, let alone a young African American woman with no prior experience in commercial real estate. However, I found a bank that was willing to do the deal but required more equity, meaning upfront capital, than I had to give. I came to the table with $100,000 but still needed $150,000 to close the deal. The solution was to find an equity partner who was very liquid and who could see the potential in the project. I then entered a business agreement with two partners. Had I done my research, I would have discovered that one of them had taken advantage of other people in the past, and I would be no different. Here was another example on how failing to do my due diligence cost me big time.

The quality of real estate investing deteriorated as lenders loaned money to people who clearly could not afford the loan, brokers convinced people to borrow way more than they could afford, and con artists found a way to use the credit and capital of the clueless to purchase a home in which they could walk away with a significant amount of cash at closing. During this time, the real estate game became the new hustle. People were willing to sell their souls to close a deal and walk away with cash. To my ignorance, my deal was nothing different. Although I secured the contract on the 119-unit building that was to be converted into a 230-unit condo development to yield over $4.5 million in profit, my equity partner found a way to cut me out of the project and take the money I had invested as well as any potential profits I stood to make from the project. This took me from a six-figure income to a zero-figure income in one fell swoop.

JM showed up at the right time – or the worst time. He came in my life like a knight on a white horse and sold me an image of himself that was exactly what I said (in my online profile) that I was looking for. Our second date was an afternoon lunch on my birthday. He brought me flowers, a teddy bear, and a card, and he admired me like I was a rare jewel. He said everything I wanted to hear. I was wide open.

It also impressed me when he knew I also had a date with someone else that evening but did not show a flicker of doubt as he encouraged me to have a good time on my "last date with the other guy." That level of confidence was a turn on. My date that evening paled in comparison to my date with JM and I found myself thinking about JM the entire evening. He was right. The date with the other guy would be the last date with other men, for a while at least, but it would also be the beginning of a nightmare I wouldn't wish on my worst enemy.

He was perfect and said all the right things. After a few weeks of dating, I shared with him what I was going through financially. Without hesitation, he stepped up and was eager to jump right in and "save" me from my situation. I wanted so badly for him to be the man I had been praying for; but I didn't stop and ask God if he was The One for me. I didn't even stop to do my due diligence...completely!

Even though I recognized that he had a slight anger problem and I would sometimes catch him in a lie, I thought that he was my 'perfect partner' by the third month that we dated. When I say perfect partner, I realize that there are no perfect people and that none of us would ever be able to find a perfect person. However, I always have believed that each person has a perfect person who compliments him or her in essential ways, and each person has that perfect person with whom he or she can build a healthy love experience. My fear and residual hurt left me unable to identify my perfect partner. He was not JM.

JM appeared to be a great father who was willing to help my kids and me during this low point in my life. He also seemed to have all his stuff together: his own home, a flourishing career, and a healthy savings account. He was a divorced father of three and he stepped right in and assumed the role of 'daddy' for my two children. I was fascinated with the idea of a man my age who was old fashioned and felt it was his responsibility as a man to protect and provide for us.

I was a single mother who had no income and was losing my home, car, and everything else I'd worked for. The stress of it all literally almost killed me.

My Brush with Death

The end of my first marriage was so painful that when I delivered our son one week after the divorce was finalized, my lung developed a blood clot that blocked oxygen from getting to my heart efficiently. This placed a strain on my heart, and three days later, I was rushed back to the hospital, dying from congestive heart failure. None of the doctors could give me any answers for three days, but I knew that it was serious. I later learned that the doctors had given up hope and did not expect me to live much longer.

I could hardly breathe or keep my eyes open when my OB/GYN came into my room in tears. She sat down on my bed, grabbed my hands, and said that there was a time when man's medicine could only go so far and then it's time to pray. She prayed with and over me and declared healing over my heart. We hugged and cried together. The next day, the cardiologist came into my room and told me how bad my heart was. He told me that I would have to stop nursing my newborn son and take several different heart medications. He told me that my heart would never be 100 percent the same again, and I would be lucky if it bounced back to 60 percent normal. My heart was enlarged and working overtime to pump blood throughout my body. The condition that I was suffering from required some people to receive a heart transplant, as the heart got progressively worse.

I, on the other hand, believed in a power greater than anything on this Earth, so I looked that doctor in the eye and told him that not only was my heart going to bounce back to 100 percent normal, but it would do it without any medications. Do not get me wrong. I am pharmaceutical sales representative and totally believe that medicine is a blessing to mankind, but I was not willing to give up nursing my son or suffer the side effects some of the medicines reportedly caused. I also had unwavering faith that my heart would heal itself.

Every day, I imagined that a white light floated around my heart, healing it inside and out, and every day, I thanked God for my healing. I would not allow anyone to stress me, and I did things that made me feel good. Within three months, I went back to that cardiologist and he ran the entire test only to find that my heart had regained 100 percent normal function. When I told him what I did to heal my heart, he said that he would give a testimony at his church that Sunday.

Now back to how I ended up falling for JM.

I followed the advice of a trusted advisor, and I filed bankruptcy to keep from losing my home. The first time I filed, it was done incorrectly, so I had to re-file. I now joined the millions of Americans who had suffered financially because of the real estate bust and I was hurt, disappointed, and bankrupt.

JM stepped in and immediately assumed my troubles. My inner guidance told me that you don't get something for nothing and my heart held back from completely falling for him. I couldn't put my finger on why. It just did not feel right.

He encouraged me to stop working a 9-to-5 so that I could work on my passion of coaching and writing books instead. I then became totally dependent on this man and eventually he held all the power.

How I Lost Myself and My Mind

Even though I showed JM that I was fully committed to him, he questioned my loyalty every single day. His insecurity lead to daily disagreements that would turn into hours long yelling matches. He would accuse me of talking to, going out with, or wanting other men and it would drive me crazy. I didn't realize that this was a common tactic for breaking a woman down and motivating her to put his needs before hers. Slowly, but surely, my confidence and self-worth diminished and eventually, I lost the strong woman I was and became who he wanted me to be. I was so busy looking at myself and trying to prove my love and loyalty to him that I didn't notice until it was too late that the house he said he owned was rented, that his bank account was nearly empty (the bank statement he showed me was fake), his sports career never took off but was a very expensive hobby, he handled money poorly hardly ever paying his bills on time - 3 cars in the duration of our time together were repossessed, and he was still married!

Although I did do a background check, saw his STD status, hired someone to follow him, and asked to see a copy of his divorce decree, I did not demand to see a *final* divorce decree. I also did not ask to speak to his ex. I accepted him leaving the room whenever she called to let him speak to his son. Eventually, I forgot to continue to press the divorce certificate issue. When I asked him if he was divorced, he assured me that he was, and in my heart and mind, I truly believed that he was legally divorced. I found out 6 months after our wedding that not only were we not legally married but that he was still married to his supposed ex-wife.

The story he told me was that the August before we met, he hired an attorney to file for a divorce on the grounds of abandonment because his wife had taken their 5-year-old son and failed to disclose their whereabouts. JM claimed that he was devastated about losing his son, and he felt that his wife no longer wanted their relationship. Having never gone through a divorce and having parents who have been married for more than 43 years, he was clueless on the divorce process, especially concerning abandonment. His trusted cousin referred him to the attorney, so he gave his cousin $4,000 to hire the attorney who would make sure the divorce was finalized. He was told that the divorce would be completed via legal notice since his wife had apparently left the state. In addition, the attorney told him that once he posted his intention to divorce her in a legal newspaper, the divorce would be final. After signing some documents, JM was assured that there was nothing for him to worry about and that the divorce would be finalized in 30 days.

According to JM, the divorce never happened because the paperwork was never filed by the attorney he paid. He told me that as a professional golfer who is constantly traveling, playing, or practicing, he trusted the people he hired would responsibly handle his affairs. Although the attorney or cousin betrayed his trust, he later recognized that his lack of follow-up ultimately created a world of problems. He shared this convincing story with tears pouring down his cheeks and my heart went out to him.

I bought that story...hook, line and sinker!

I wanted to believe I was too smart to actually marry someone who would be willing to commit bigamy. However, the truth is I believe that he did know he was still married and that he deliberately lied when he said that he was divorced. First, I later discovered that he knew that his wife moved back to Chicago where her family lived. Second, who files for divorce without seeing a judge and happily collecting the divorce decree? Lastly, I asked him about showing me the divorce decree so many times in the beginning of the relationship that if he really felt that his attorney "took care of it" he would have at least thought to reach out to the attorney and inquire about his paperwork. Also, after living with him for a little over a year, I learned that he had a very serious issue with telling the truth. Needless to say, I did it again! I entered into a relationship with a Don't Wanter and it nearly cost my sanity.

Unfortunately, people are not always honest. Had I completed the entire checklist, I would have discovered that he was still married. Had I known this in the beginning, he would not have gotten past Go. Had I discovered this several months before our wedding, he would have received the boot. Had I slowed down, prayed, got myself together, and put on a clear pair of glasses, I would have seen JM for what he was – a con artist and a Don't Wanter.

How I Found Out He Was Married

The day before Thanksgiving, as we prepared to pack for a trip to Florida to visit my family, I opened my *YouTube* channel to check the comments. I noticed a message under my wedding video that said, "JM is a bigamist, and he is married to my best friend." Under that message, I saw several other posts along those lines from what appeared to be his ex-wife and her friends. Surprised and outraged, I asked him what they were talking about. He didn't even try to lie to me.

A disheartened look came over his face before he broke down crying and he told me that when he went to apply for our marriage certificate, a court clerk said that he would not be able to file it until he produced a divorce decree. Evidently, the system showed that he was still legally married. He said that when he went through the court records to find his final decree, he could not find anything. He panicked and tried to call his cousin to get the name of the attorney who supposedly handled the divorce. He could not get him on the phone, but in a twisted turn of events, he found out after our wedding that his cousin died on the morning of our wedding. He now had no documents, no witnesses and no divorce. He somehow convinced the pastor to marry us without a certificate anyhow, and I entered into this marriage unaware that the whole thing was a sham.

At least he put some serious thought and creativity into his story. As I read this 10 years later, I cannot believe that I allowed this to happen. I cannot believe that I was so blinded by love. I want to stress the importance of keeping your wits about you, asking God to guide your dating choices and reveal to you if the person you are dating is The One. I want to stress that when you are under the fog of infatuation, right then is the time to make sure you execute your comprehensive due diligence!

According to JM, he went behind my back in an effort to "fix" the situation. He hired an attorney without telling me and tried to negotiate a divorce from his wife that would be resolved as soon as possible. In his mind, there was no harm done if the divorce was completed without me ever knowing the "glitch" had occurred. What JM did not plan for was his ex-wife's reaction when she discovered that their marriage was not legally dissolved. She launched a public campaign to tell anyone who would listen that I was married to her husband and that our marriage was not legal. She posted messages online that said he left her and their son for me.

Karma came for me and she came with a vengeance! I believe I launched that cycle when I stayed in a relationship with a married man for too long after discovering he was married, and now, years later, I found myself deceived into a marrying an already married man and accused of the worst things a 'relationship expert' can be accused of.

I hated that I had opened the door for this kind of attack. I was aggravated that this woman could still claim him as her husband even though she'd left him two years prior. I didn't know that she left because he was abusing her the way that he eventually abused me. I was hurt and pissed that he did not tell me the truth from the beginning. He begged me not to leave, and not only did I stay, I publicly defended him because I made a vow before God. We had already started to build a life together as husband and wife. My kids were well adjusted to our home, their schools, and this life. How do you just undo a permanent commitment you made in front of family, friends, and God? I'd made a commitment that this time I intended to keep.

One day I will write a book about healing one's wounds so to attract a wholesome relationship instead of an abusive one. In that book I will share details of what I endured in my relationship with JM. It was beyond what you probably could imagine I would tolerate. Because I know that there are women who are hurting right now and this book may be an inspiration to get out of an abusive relationship or at least avoid one, I will share with you how I was able to eventually walk away.

As I stated before, JM and I argued and fought a lot! We fought every day, to be exact, and it was about the same thing: Who I was talking to on the phone and what other guy was I messing with. We tried counseling. After several weeks of counseling with my church pastor, I revealed that he lied to me and married me while still being married. This was a shock to my pastor. As I sat there in a fog asking her if God approved of me leaving my husband if he deceived me so badly and how much I did not want to break my vows, she started talking. I didn't really hear her, and just kept going on about my feelings of guilt and conflict. My pastor was calling my name. The third time she called my name I looked her in her eyes and she said "Shay! You are NOT married!" She said it again and something clicked in my head. It was almost like I woke up! I looked over at him and I could see the fear in his eyes because he knew then it was only a matter of time until I was gone.

Eventually, I got tired. I got tired of not having any money. I got tired of him using money to control me. I got tired of him feeling like it was my job as a woman to clean the house, cook his food, stay home, and take care of his affairs. I got tired of fighting, crying, and feeling like I had to constantly prove myself to him. I got tired

of being less than who I was. As I explained in the 'Don't Wanters'
chapter, one day, during one of these arguments, my phone rang. I
am not sure how her ringtone in my phone changed, but it did, and
the ring tone was *Kiss of Life* by Sade. It was my best friend. I sent
the call to voicemail since I was in the middle of one of our
marathon shouting matches. Since the ring tone was a love song,
he immediately assumed it was another man and demanded to see
my phone. This time, I said, "No." He yelled at me, called me all
sorts of foul names and even jumped on top of me trying to grab
the phone. My best friend called back and this time I answered
without putting the phone to my ear and she heard him
threatening to get his gun as he yelled and stomped around the
house. I heard her yelling at me to call the police. I jumped up and
ran into the closet and called 911. I filed for a restraining order and
with no money, no job, and no source of income, I walked away.

To Forgive or Not to Forgive

My life was a nightmare when I was with JM. Nothing went right,
and it seemed like there was a bad luck cloud over my head. I was
attacked from every angle. A nanny he hired wrongfully sued me.
Opportunities constantly slipped through my fingers and everything
that could go wrong, went wrong. This was also a sign that I was
with the wrong person and on the wrong path. If you are with
someone who seems to bring a lot of baggage to the table and now
you are dealing with drama in your life, it is a sign that you are
probably with the wrong person. Once you discover you've made
the wrong choice, don't stay to prove a point and torture yourself.
Leave!

Break-Ups

Break-ups get such a bad rap, but the point of life is to grow,
discover and learn. You attract the people who come into your life
because you are vibrating at that frequency level. Remember the
Law of Attraction. When you elevate your vibration, they will no
longer fit in your world. This is what is supposed to happen.

Sometimes we meet stepping-stones on the road to attracting The One. Abraham Hicks calls this deliberate creation. Often you have to know what you don't want in order to attract what you do want into your life. The name of the game is to eventually reach a point when you stop beating up on yourself and forgive and love yourself. It is at this point when you know you deserve to be loved and reach a place where you can attract a wholesome love that matches your vibration of expectation.

It took a while to discover why I went through that experience. It took even longer to forgive myself. I never pretended to be perfect. I taught women what not to do because of the mistakes that I made and used my life as a handbook on what not to do when dating. This drama was downright embarrassing. I was embarrassed because I felt I should have known better. I questioned how in the world this could happen to me and I was mad at myself for not following my own advice.

Unforgiveness motivated me to walk away from relationship coaching, TV, and everything that came with helping people find love. I wasn't the same and I just could not forgive myself for letting people down. In a way, this experience was an ego-check that reminded me that just because I knew a lot on the subject of relationships, I was not immune to mistakes or restricted from self-forgiveness. I also had a lot of healing to do.

At first, this situation crippled me. I felt helpless and angry all the time, and I couldn't see the lesson. Then, one day I woke up and decided that I would no longer choose to allow the situation to control me. What I did not realize at the time was that this experience was only making me stronger and building a character within me that would never have developed had this not happened to me.

I had survived being shot in the chest at the age of 17 in a drive-by shooting; a car accident in which a friend fell asleep at the wheel and the car flipped over five times until it landed in a tree; congestive heart failure after the birth of my son; and a minor heart attack at the age of 31. After all of this, I was surely not going to let the end of my sham-marriage and the embarrassment of being conned by a married man break me. Eventually, I made peace with my past, healed my pain, and attracted my soulmate.

Lessons to be Learned

Many people have so much baggage that even if Jesus showed up, they would see the devil because the lens of their perception is jaded. They see everything from the perspective of the father who was not there; the friend who betrayed them; or the man/woman who left them. Therefore, they are unable to exist in the reality of the moment and see things for what they are. This is the reason why it is important to take time to heal those unresolved issues and to use our relationships as the barometer of what healing is still necessary. Buddhists say that the person who drives you the craziest is your master teacher. Whatever bothers you most about your spouse or significant other may be something within you that you need to work on as well.

When a woman falls for a man, she is emotionally attached to him, and these emotions plus biological reactions cause her to override all common sense and put her guard down. Most women make this mistake because we are emotional. We base our perception of reality on our feelings and believe what people tell us. Most of us are unaware that in the beginning, when love causes our hormones to rage, we are vulnerable and should avoid making major life decisions.

What happened to my family and me could happen to anyone. After all that I have shared, some of you are still thinking that none of this could happen to you. It is not my goal to scare you, but to impress upon you that doing your homework by completing a full background check on your potential mate can spare your heart, protect your wallet, and even save your life. There are hundreds of women and their children who let their guard down too soon, only to end up with a first-class ticket to the graveyard. I recommend that if you do not believe me, Google "stepfather murders" or rent the movie *Stepfather*. In this movie, the man is deranged and kills the family of the women he draws into his web of lies. There are women who torment themselves every day because their own children were the victims of their own poor judgment after they trusted someone who was a murderer or pedophile. There are evil people out here who are so convincing you would never suspect that they might be capable of harming you or your children.

Many single women with children date less, so they are more likely to crave companionship. Therefore, predatory men find them to be easy targets. Also, because many single mothers spend so much time and energy focusing on their children, they often neglect their love lives and do not see the need to study the new dating atmosphere and how to enter it armed with the knowledge of how to protect themselves and recognize a man's intentions. Many single women place the majority of their focus on their careers, friends or hanging out.

As a single mother, I knew how important it was to learn what I didn't know and select the right kind of man who would be great for my kids and myself. Nothing could be worse than discovering you could have prevented a tragedy simply by doing your homework. I suffered being stalked and humiliated for several months because I failed to do what I am encouraging you to do. Learn from my mistake and do better!

Chapter 11.
Taking It to The Next Level
Using Old School Rules

You followed the advice in this book and attracted a great guy who is into you. Now your job is to determine if he is really the man for you and whether he is worthy of going to the next level with you. Your job is also to enjoy yourself and learn more about what you want in the right partner. This type of relationship often starts out hot and heavy and seems to mimic a romantic love story, but you must maintain alignment with the Law of Attraction in order to be clear if he is really The One.

Many women don't date because they are uncertain about how to be confident in a relationship. They fear being hurt, messing up a great relationship, or the possible end of a relationship with someone who initially made them happy. In order to take your relationship to the next level, while avoiding being disappointed, you have to play your cards right. Try to keep your eyes open and look for the signs that he is really starting to fall for you. The goal is to set his heart on fire for you. Remember, men love a challenge, but they are not thrilled with Fort Knox. Try to be balanced and allow him to nibble at the carrot you dangle in front of him. Do not try too hard to force things to click between you. Allow it to flow together on its own. There is a blessing in every relationship – even the ones that did not work. Trust that the right one will work.

The following are common old school rules taught by our grandmothers that have worked for generations and will work for you if you work them. So please, don't deviate from these rules by breaking every single one of them and think that you will be the exception to the rule and end up with Prince Charming. If he is your perfect partner, I guarantee you that he will be ok with working for your love and trust. In fact, he will welcome the fun challenge while praying that you never get too easy and hoping that you will always keep him on his toes.

Grandma's Rules

The phone is a powerful communication weapon that can make or break the relationship, so use it wisely. Here are some rules about telephoning:

Rule #1: He should be the one making the first few phone calls.

If he offers his number, give him yours. If he doesn't call, NEXT!

Rule #2: The first time a man calls you, you should be so busy that you have to call him back.

Rule #3: Put the phone down. He should be the one doing most of the calling.

You are a DIVA, and a DIVA has a life. When you have a life, you do not have time to call a man too often.

Rule #4: Do not stay on the phone longer than 15 minutes per call.

The phone is for setting up face-to-face time. The days of staying on the phone all night and listening to each other breathe should have ended in high school.

Rule #5: Block your number when you call him.

In the beginning of the courtship block your number because he may not answer the phone. If he doesn't answer the phone, you are not left wondering if he is going to call you back or why he didn't call back. If he doesn't answer, you can simply unblock your number and call back later – but only one additional time. The ball remains in your court. When calling from your home phone (there are still a few people out there with landlines), you do not want him to have your home number for a while because he can use the number to Mapquest where you live — a big no-no in the dating world of single women.

Rule #6: Avoid a textual relationship.

Who was the genius who invented texting? By the time you finish typing into your phone the entire book about what you wanted to say you could have picked up the phone and simply said what you had to say.

Texting has changed the way we communicate in relationships. It was created for convenience, but people have turned it into their sole mode of communication. What is even worse is that men with bad intentions, or who really may not be serious about a woman, have abused texting to control and limit the amount of personal interaction with that woman.

There was a time in history when boys were forced to be men and overcome their fear of rejection by approaching a woman and asking her for a dance or a date. There was a time when men had to pick up the phone and maintain a conversation with a woman as an expression that he really cared about her or was interested in getting to know her better. The lack of certain advanced technology bred better quality men and separated the boys from the men, or the serious guy from the Player.

As technology advances, it appears it has deteriorated the dating process and weakened the connection between men and women. The purpose of the courting phase is to allow a man who is serious about a woman to demonstrate his intentions and potential love for her through his actions. While dating, it is a man's behavior that increases trust and sense of security in a woman. The more a woman is able to trust a man, the more she is able to let go and genuinely love and care for him.

Unfortunately, many women settle for a man's unwillingness to show her that he is serious about her and fall prey to getting played. Women can avoid the heartbreak if they remember that there are some things that will remain consistent throughout the end of time. One of those things is that if a man really cares for you, he will naturally desire to do what makes you happy. A man can only confirm that his beloved is happy and that he was successful at making her happy by checking up on her by means of personal contact either in person or over the phone. A sweet text here and there peppered throughout the day is fine, but he receives joy in hearing her voice or seeing her face.

If you must text, it should only be used for short, unimportant, messages. It should not be used to set or cancel a date. It should be used to let the person know that you are just leaving the house and on the way to the date. It should not be used to have an argument. It should be used if you want to send a "hi" or sweet messages during the day to let your loved one know that you are thinking of him. The sweet nothing texts should not start until at least a month into the relationship.

If a man refuses to pick up the phone and call you, chances are that he is just not 'feeling' you enough. The "hey baby" text followed by "you are the most beautiful woman in the world" absent of a follow-up call by the end of the day is evidence that he a) is not serious about a relationship with you, b) may be committed to someone else, or c) is a Player using the convenient method of texting to carry out his player game.

Texting can be a bit tricky. Some of us ladies believe that we can text a man all the time as long as we are not calling him all the time. WRONG! Over-initiating contact via text is just as bad as calling too often. If you allow him to communicate too much through texting, you will hate the impersonal nature of your relationship in the long run.

Daily phone calls may not be realistic in the beginning of a relationship, but I would suggest that you end textual relationships before they begin by being clear with what you are willing to tolerate from the start. If a man is over using text messaging to communicate his feelings for you, simply share with him that you would prefer phone calls over a text. If he continues the behavior, cut him loose and keep it moving because he is wasting your time and unwilling to do what it takes to demonstrate to you why he deserves your heart.

As your relationship progresses, Grandma has advice for how to proceed:

Rule #7: Do not say "I love you" first.

The man should be the first one to reveal any intense feelings. You do not want to scare him or get hurt by revealing your feelings before he has had a chance to develop or realize his feelings. It may be erupting inside of you, but whatever you do, keep it to yourself and let him make the first "I love you" confession. In addition, saying "I love you" means something much more than simply having romantic feelings, or being 'in love'. It's a declaration of commitment, which can scare a man who is not ready.

Rule #8: Never allow the relationship to turn into a 'friends with benefits' game.

With the turn of the last century came the women's revolution, which I am not sure was totally beneficial to our vaginas. Today's woman's sense of freedom is so strong that she can now walk up to a man, ask him for a drink, and have no problem having sex with him on the first night if she chooses. I have already explained in Chapter 7 that you should keep your legs closed and focus on setting his heart on fire for you first. I am encouraging you to value your vagina and everything it represents.

Ladies, your vaginas stand for power, value, and respect. Too many women are opening their legs, hearts and minds and allowing any man who shows them attention to enjoy the golden treasures between their legs. The desire to avoid being alone is so strong that it has women doing many desperate things in the name of love. If you do not love yourself, how can you expect anyone else to truly love you for who you really are? When you love yourself, you place a high value on yourself and demand a high standard of respect in return. A woman who values her 'v' would not open her heart to just any man unless he showed her that he deserved it. A woman who values her 'v' would never chase a man or take less than what she deserves from him. A woman who values her 'v' would be extremely selective when it comes to allowing a man to have her heart, mind and body. Lastly, a woman who values her 'v' knows that she cannot be sure a man deserves her unless she gives herself time to get to know him and build a foundation of friendship first.

Friendship is the beginning, not the qualifier for giving a man your body. If he still has the title of 'friend', he is automatically disqualified from having sex with you. If he has not yet committed to you and made you his girlfriend or potential wife, then what makes him worthy of the greatest gift you can give him? If he fails to give you a title but continues to sleep with you as he introduces you as his friend, then rest assured, he is sleeping with his other 'friends' to whom he has no moral ties either. In essence, he enjoys all of the benefits of having 'friends' while you are left hoping your friend will eventually see you as more than just a booty call. "Why should he buy the cow, when he already gets the milk for free?"

Your 'v' is not a glass of water to be given to any thirsty man looking for a drink. Your vagina is gold and should be treated as such. Loneliness and the desperation to be loved are as destructive a combination as driving while under the influence. Casual sex will never be the substitute for finding true love, so choose today to never give a 'friend' your 'benefits'. Make sure that before you open your heart to a man who showers you with great words, he supports his words with actions and earns your affection. If you get yourself together first and fall in love with who you are, it will become easy to set a high standard, which will increase the quality of prospects that come your way.

I suggest waiting until marriage before having any type of sex with a man. I know that many women fear that if they do not have sex, the man will get it from somewhere else. If a man is really feeling you, he will wait on you and still want to marry you. If he does not have good intentions for you anyway, he will cheat and have sex with someone else whether you sleep with him or not. However, I do understand that in the real world, many people just do not wait. It is tough to fight the pull of horniness. So, if you are going to have sex before saying, "I do," do not have sex with him for at least three months. Within this time, you two should have gone through the three stages of dating (please refer to *Mars and Venus on a Date* by John Gray) and your relationship should have reached the commitment status before you become intimate with him. For some couples, it takes a couple of months. For others, it takes longer, but the point is that you must give the relationship a chance to develop roots and grow beyond the uncertainty phase every relationship starts with. The uncertainty phase is the phase when you both start to question if he or she is The One or if you want to pursue the relationship any further. It is for this reason that reaching the commitment phase before giving up the goodies is very important to the future success of your relationship. If you can't hold out, I have a contingency plan for you that we will discuss in Chapter 14.

Rule #9: No one-night stands EVER!

Would you ever put a spoon in your mouth that a stranger just pulled out of their mouth? Even if you wear a condom, you are still exchanging fluids and germs with a person you know absolutely nothing about. YUCK!

Ladies, your goal is to be a prize to your man. You do not want him to think that you are easy, and if you did this with him, you probably have done this with other men. An easy catch is an easy throwback, and this is true for both sexes. If your goal is to get your rocks off, then open your sex toy box and wait for The One instead of finding some random guy with whom you could never fall in love. Most women develop attachments and waste their time and energy trying to accommodate their horniness. It is better to wait than to have regrets.

Rule #10: Let him ask you out on dates.

Most hard-working women know how to take charge and make things happen. This is great at work or at home if you are a mom, but in the dating world, it spells disaster. Let him be the man and initiate the dates. When a man is into you, he wants to see you and be around you. If he wants to be around you, he will invite you out. Make sure that he books weekend dates by Wednesday. He should value your plans and time if he is serious about you.

Rule #11: Demand respect from him at all times.

He should not feel comfortable cursing around you, calling women bitches (which is a deal breaker, by the way), and sending text messages while on a date with you or talking on the phone at dinner. I can't emphasize it enough: Do not settle for less than you deserve and always stand by your standards. A man will meet your standards if he wants you badly enough and if he is worthy. If he doesn't want to meet your standards, kick him to the streets.

Rule #12: Do not introduce him to your family and children until he earns it.

You should wait at least six months before introducing him to your family, especially if you have had more than two failed relationships within the past year. That way, if you do make it that long as a couple, your family will take him more seriously, and he will respect and appreciate them more because it took him so long to enter such an intimate part of your life.

Rule #13: Show your smarts.

Men get bored with ditsy, unintelligent women. Some women dumb down their intelligence because they believe that this will make them appear more attractive to a man. This thinking cannot be any further from the truth. Men find intelligent women sexy. Good men love to have their minds challenged and to be able to learn something new from the lady in their lives. They also love to brag about your drive, your goals and accomplishments, and especially your intelligence. So, keep your wits about you, and lose the ignorance.

Rule #14: Let him know when he is wrong.

Men do not like weak women who don't speak up when something is wrong. As a matter of fact, he will even test her to see how she will respond if he suspects she is a pushover. Men love to be challenged to become better. This turns them on. If he thinks that it is okay to belch in public, you need to be the one to set him straight, but in a DIVA, tactful way. Remember, you are not his mother, but you are going to become his best friend, and best friends are honest with each other and bring out the best in each other.

Rule #15: Praise him when he does something that you really like.

You can mold a man to be and do anything you desire, as long as you have a man who is really into you. If he is moldable, you can mold him without him even knowing it. In fact, he will enjoy the process of being molded if you do it right.

In the 1800's, a scientist did an experiment in which he took a dog and would ring a bell whenever the dog's food was placed before him. The dog began to anticipate eating whenever he heard the bell ring and would automatically salivate at the sound. The dog became so conditioned to eating after the sound of a bell that whenever he heard a bell ring, whether the food appeared or not, he would salivate. The scientist trained the dog to produce an automatic reaction to a stimulus. The automatic response was the salivating, and the stimulus was the bell.

Like in the experiment, you are the scientist, and the man is the dog. Your affirmation or praise is the bell that motivates his good deeds. You are going to condition him to the point that whenever he does something wonderful for you, he will get an emotional high. Men love praise, and whenever a man receives praise from his beloved, he gets a high. If you praise your man and make him feel great every time he does something nice for you, he will automatically do wonderful things and receive the high even before you recognize him for that good deed. This method of training, not changing your man, is way more effective than the nagging approach.

Starting a relationship sometimes feels like tap dancing. Remember to have fun and don't stress about whether it will work out in the long term or not, because you know that you will eventually attract The One. The name of the game is to learn more about yourself and what you can and cannot live with in your life partner. I encourage you to follow certain rules because your natural instincts will often have you sabotaging a potentially great relationship or behaving in ways that make you feel less than who you are. Enjoy the ride but follow the rules and you will eventually reach your destination to love!

Chapter 12.
The Magic Bullets

This chapter is worth more than all the gold that you could possibly possess. I will give you the tried and true secrets of how to make any man with whom you have connected or have chemistry, fall head over heels for you.

I learned most of this information from the famous life coach Anthony "Tony" Robbins. I respect his work and would recommend that you attend his seminars or purchase his audio material. When I attended his *Get the Power* and *Date with Destiny* seminars, my life changed significantly. What I learned from this genius was that we all have six basic needs that dictate our behaviors, actions, and reactions to all of life's experiences. A woman can learn how to meet these needs and cause her man to never need or desire another woman again.

Special note before I proceed: There must be a mutual connection first for the information I am about to reveal to be effective.

The Six Human Needs in Relationships

The six human needs in relationships vary in order of importance for each individual. However, everyone has the same six basic human needs. One need might motivate the actions of one individual more than it motivates someone else. It is important that you learn the particular order and extent of these needs for your partner, and anchor yourself to those needs. The needs are as follows:

Certainty

The need to feel certain that people are who they say they are and that you can trust they will not betray you in any way or hurt you. In order to meet this need, you must feel certain that you can depend on another person. The men who are primarily motivated by this need would prefer an honest woman who is stable financially and mentally and is not attracted to him because of his social or financial status. He knows that when you tell him something, he can take it to the bank because you always keep it real. Your personality is the same no matter who you are around, and you do not have 'crazy' inconsistent tendencies. He wants to know that if he ever needed you that he could trust you would be there for him even if he lost all his money or social status. These men are big on marrying a loyal woman they can trust.

To meet a man's need for certainty, be honest, consistent, and loyal. When you do decide to be committed, you must never cheat on him. To this man, having a 'good girl' he considers a prize is important because not many men have been able to conquer you. This means everything to him in a relationship. If he ever catches you in a lie, you will be potentially knocked out of the contender's spot of becoming his wife.

Uncertainty

Some people have the need for unpredictability or variety. We all desire certainty, but the need for uncertainty (surprises) is equally important. Just think about it. If you repeatedly watched an action movie, it would become boring because you would know and predict everything that happens. This is the same in dating! That's why you need to keep an edge and a level of mystery about you. Do not reveal everything about yourself all at once. Don't make yourself available to him any time he wants you. Do not engage in sexual activity with him every time you are together. Be a challenge to him on occasion or wear lingerie sometimes – this will satisfy that need for uncertainty. Men who are big on the need for uncertainty desire women who are independent (can stand on their own two feet but are not so independent that they don't need a man), intelligent, and strong-minded. To these men, a woman who is always busy but still makes time for him, is a major turn on. He enjoys being kept on his toes by the object of his affection.

Love/Connection

The need to experience love and connection with another individual is essential to all human beings. Men desire and fall in love just as much, if not more so, than women. The need for love and connection is so strong and addictive that some men jump from one relationship to the next because they are addicted to the high of the honeymoon phase. The honeymoon phase is the first six months of a relationship when everything is wonderful and blissful, and both parties are walking on a cloud. Once this 'in love' phase begins to wane, the couple must *choose* to love each other if they see something in each other worth loving. When you choose to love a person after seeing the good, the bad and the ugly, true love has a chance to emerge.

To appeal to this need, form a bond with your partner that will be considered unlike any connection he has ever experienced. Mirroring and mimicking will help to facilitate this feeling. When you have things in common and often hear yourselves saying, "Me too," the love/connection feeling is growing. When you can spiritually connect and truly "feel" each other, he will be hooked, I promise. When a man falls in love, he falls hard, and it takes a while for him to get over heartbreak. For this reason, it takes him longer to let down his guard and allow himself to be in love.

Growth

Whether spiritually, intellectually, emotionally, or physically, everyone has the basic need to grow and improve for the better. When a man feels that he is better because of you and that you make him a better man, this fulfills his need for growth. It is for this reason that strong, intelligent women who stimulate men intellectually and push them to grow in areas in which they are weak are more desirable than passive women who never challenge their man when he is wrong.

To meet this need, find out his goals and dreams. Learn his insecurities, and subtly, slowly work on those areas by encouraging him to become better and reach for his goals. See him as the greatest version of himself while loving him as he is, where he is. Dream with him and tell him how you can imagine and see him accomplishing his goals. Go a step further and describe to him what this would look like. Never accept mediocrity from him if you know that he can do better. Be careful not to become his mother or a nag! When he comes to you with a life or career challenge, do not make the mistake of offering him advice. Simply encourage him to not give up and tell him you trust that he will figure it out. If he wants a pity party, cry with him if necessary and allow him to see that you understand why he feels the way he does, but you will not participate in the pity party with him for long.

Significance

The need to feel important is strong in most men. To have this need met, one must feel a sense of power and control over their environment and certain circumstances. For instance, many men are workaholics because when they become the best at what they do, they receive accolades on the job. This fulfills their need for significance. When a man feels he is important to you and that you respect him as a man, this need is being met. Lack of a feeling of significance is the number one reason why men say that they left their wife for another woman. These men almost always say that it was because of the way the mistress made them feel. They usually say that she made them feel as if they could accomplish anything and that they were important. Most women, when they get their man, get comfortable and stop appealing to this major need.

Now breathe, I know that last sentence ticked off lots of you. However, this is the truth, and instead of getting mad, attempt to use this information to secure a better man than the one who left. When you affirm your man and recognize his strengths, it allows him to feel significant. To meet this need in your man, let him know how proud you are of him for X, Y, Z. Whatever X, Y, Z is, state those things specifically. When he comes home, get off the phone and call your girlfriend back later. Iron his clothes and cook him a meal once in a while, especially if that is NOT your thing to do. I hate domestic work, but I knew that when I wanted to cook, clean, and iron my man's clothes, I was in love. He recognized this and appreciated me for it.

When you say nice things about your man to his friends, co-workers, or family when he's not around, this also helps to make him feel significant. It is important to mention that you must never, ever humiliate or disrespect your man in public or private, call him out of his name, or put your hands on him. When you tear down a man's feeling of significance, you are left with only a shell of a man, which is worse than not having anyone. Start the relationship off right and agree early on that respect, by both parties, must be maintained at all times.

Contribution

The need to feel as though you are making a difference in the life of your loved one is important. This need is the opposite of the need for growth. With contribution, you are the one helping him to grow and be better. With the need for growth, he is the one who is sewing into you and helping you be and do and think better. Men are also protectors and problem-solvers by nature. This explains why they react the way they do when you run to them with a problem. They are quick to tell you how to fix the situation when all you really want is a listening ear. Most of us desire to make a difference in the world, our community, and our loved one's lives, and we want to make these things better.

To meet a man's need for contribution, he must feel that he is also making a positive impact in your life. To help him meet that need, walk the fine line of allowing him to be your lover, best friend, and father figure. Most importantly, allow him to feel like he is your hero. This is the barrier of many independent, career-minded, successful women. They do not understand that it is not their success or money that intimidates men from marrying them, it is their inability to allow their man to feel as though he is needed. Keep your money in your bank account and tone down that "I got it going on" air about you. Even if you don't need his help if your car breaks down, call him up in distress and let him pay for the tow truck and help fix the situation. Give him a chance to show you that he is really into you by being your hero. No one is asking you to be ashamed of your success. Just be wise and figure out ways to allow a man to see where and how he can fit into your life without coming off as if you are high maintenance.

In addition, allow him to feel as though his presence makes you better as a person. Maybe it is the advice he gives you, the way he encourages you, or the way he puts you in your place when you need it. Wherever you can allow him to contribute to your life, let him. Sometimes saying "Yes dear," when he tells you something to do or not to do and actually doing or not doing that thing, will meet his need for contribution.

These basic needs are simple, but they are very powerful when understood and utilized. The more needs that you satisfy and anchor, the greater the possibility of a lasting love. Remember, love is like a bank, and the six needs are accounts. The more you deposit into these accounts, the stronger your portfolio. Make sure that you learn what needs motivate your partner most and in what order. Meet these needs, and he will try to satisfy you in every way.

Chakra Firing

Chakra firing is one of the most powerful methods to help grow a man's love for you. Doing chakra firing means that you will open yourself up on a spiritual plane with the pure intention of sending love energy to the other person. Chakra firing is completely selfless but also benefits you when done correctly. It can only work when you have good intentions and the person receiving the sending is already into you in the same way. Understand that whomever you fire upon, will become connected to you emotionally and spiritually. Make sure that you know beyond a shadow of a doubt that he is someone it will be safe to be connected to in this way or you may end up hurt and have a hard time moving on if necessary.

The body has seven main energy centers (chakras), which correlate with the seven colors of the rainbow. *Chakra* (pronounced sha-kra) is the Sanskrit word for 'wheel'. When you go to see an acupuncturist as a holistic approach for treating a specific illness, he or she is placing a needle through minor chakras throughout your body in an effort to heal you or help your body produce a particular reaction. When your chakras or energy centers are rotating smoothly, your mind, body, and spirit work as they should. For the purpose of this activity, we will focus on the Heart Chakra, which is located within the heart. When activated, it produces a great sense of connectivity and love.

The best way to increase your chakra firing ability is to do the chakra firing meditation that I created to help you. It walks you through this process in a meditation fashion.

Meditation Exercise

- Start by facing the man whom you care for deeply and imagine that your heart starts to glow with a bright green light that floats above your heart.

- Imagine that as this green light grows, your heart power increases. Feel this energy growing within your body and feel the love fill every cell within you.

- Picture that you have an invisible wand that you can fire at your own free will. Imagine that your green light travels through your wand and fires directly at his green light located over his heart. Like a gun, you fire a surge of energy to his heart that is nothing but love, peace, and blessings for him.

ﻉ He will feel the energy but not know where it is coming from. If he cares for you already, this will only intensify his feelings for you and make him feel more connected to you without really knowing why. This is not something you want to play with or take lightly, so use it wisely and only on those who are worthy.

Secrets Every Man Wants a Woman to Know but Would NEVER Tell Her!

While conducting my experiments and research, I discovered some things about men that have been extremely surprising to many women. I will share some of these secrets with you to remove some of the mystery men seem to have about them that confuses and baffles a lot of women. This information can help prevent you from throwing away a good relationship or making excuses for a man who is a Don't Wanter. Read for wisdom, not manipulation and allow the knowledge to improve your comfortability with dating the opposite sex.

Here are some truths that you may not know about men but that you'll need to understand them:

- Men are not complicated.
- Men are more sensitive than women think and can be hurt more easily than women. Don't let the tough exterior fool you. They are just better than women at hiding this.
- He really doesn't want the chase to end too soon, especially if he really likes you.
- Just wait before having sex with him.
- He really, really, really wants to impress you. That's why he talks so much about himself on the first date!
- It makes his heart melt when you smile while looking into his eyes.
- Deep down he is scared that he will not be good enough and because of this, you may not like or love him.

- If he is a good guy, he would rather pull his eyes out than to argue with you or see you cry.
- If he is really into you, he wants to provide for you and make you happy.
- He wants to be loved for who he is, not what he can do for you.
- Your words do hurt him, and he feels rejected when you are mad at him.
- He needs to have time to himself sometimes.
- He must feel like the man in the relationship in order to be a good man to you.
- His greatest fear is to be disrespected in public by his woman. Don't EVER do it!
- He really doesn't know how he feels right now. Just give him time to think.
- He must have space to watch the game.
- It doesn't mean that he doesn't love you if he doesn't pay attention to you while you are talking during the game.
- Your confidence turns him on. Your insecurity and neediness turn him off.
- He lies because he is terrified of what your reaction may be — period!
- Yes, he did notice the bombshell with the nice butt, double "D" sized breasts and long legs, 10 seconds before you did.
- If he says he loves you, and you feel his sincerity, he is probably telling the truth.
- Just believe him and receive his love.
- He is not listening when you are fussing or nagging, no matter how loud you yell.
- He does not care about the name brand of the outfit, just how sexy it makes you look.
- Men talk about the opposite sex more than women do.
- Men take longer to get over heartbreak than women do.
- Right now, he is probably thinking about sex. Men need sex like fish need water.

❥

- He will come back if you give him space when he pulls away.
- He doesn't call because either he doesn't want to appear needy (beginning of the relationship); he is not really feeling you (during and towards end of relationship); or is tied physically or emotionally to someone else (you two have no relationship).

Chapter 13.
You Have the Man

No feeling is more powerful than the 'in love' feeling. Most individuals describe being in love as if they are uncontrollably driven to be with and please another person. They give to that person typically without thought, restraint, or motive. In the eyes of those who feel they are in love their beloved can do no wrong.

The body is a complex system of cells and organs whose actions are often fueled by invisible chemical reactions, and it is important to realize what invisible events occur within the body to cause this uncontrollable behavior. Many people are unaware that the brain releases many hormones and chemicals involved with producing this in love feeling. For this reason, making a major commitment to the object of your affection is extremely dangerous while being under the influence of the chemical addiction of love.

According to Donatella Marazziti of the University of Pisa, the early stages of romantic love begin with the release of adrenaline and phenylethylamine (or PEA, also present in small amounts in chocolate). These hormones are ignited when two people find themselves increasingly attracted to each other. Marazziti also discovered that the early stages of being in love are associated with a high level of serotonin, which causes a euphoria that drives people to obsessively think about, want to be around, and consistently reflect on the special moments spent with their beloved. More interestingly, Marazziti's research discovered that when people are in love, there is a decrease in the male hormone testosterone in men and an increase of testosterone in women. Testosterone is linked to aggression and sexual desire and is the hormone that causes men in the uterus to become male instead of remaining female.

What all of this means is that our actions are no longer 'our' actions once we are under the influence of being in love. We are under the influence of the side effect of a chemical process occurring within the body. This chemical process occurs for one reason and one reason only, to maintain the existence of human life. If man and woman did not have this chemical process occurring within them, the human race would soon become extinct because the desire to mate would cease. You may think that your decisions while being drunk on the 'in love' feeling are your own, however, they are not. Often, these decisions are not the same decision you would have made once the euphoria wears off. According to Marazziti's study, the 'in love' euphoria subsides on average after two years. For some, the romantic feeling of being in love wears off within 9 months, but for others, it takes many years.

You will know when you have passed the 'in love' stage when your beloved is no longer the person you evaluate through rose-colored glasses. In other words, he is no longer the person who can do no wrong. The good news is that real, true, lasting love does exist, but it is not achieved overnight.

When true love shows up, a conscious choice is made to make a commitment to love this person in spite of their 'unlovable' side. True love knocks at your door when you begin wondering if this is the person with whom you want to spend the rest of your life. You may even want to leave that person because of the undesirable qualities you can now see clearly. You beckon to true love's call when you decide to stay with the person not because you are hormonally addicted to them, but because, overall, this person brings out the best in you and is good for you. Only when this happens should you say, "I do," because, at that moment, a marriage now has a chance of thriving and withstanding the test of time. Basically, the development of true love takes time, and it is not until real love enters the relationship – not its look-alike cousin, infatuation – that one should make any major decisions with one's life, especially getting married.

Vulnerability is the seedbed for love. Without it, true love will never occur. Still, wisdom and common sense should regulate the direction of a potential love connection because even people who love you can come to take you for granted if you are not careful.

Here are some relationship rules that will help you remain open but not lose yourself totally while in love.

Relationship Rules

Rule #1: Do not spend too much time with him.

You have a life; remember? Hanging out once or twice during the week and once on the weekend is more than enough in the beginning of the relationship.

Rule #2: Be unpredictable.

If he calls you every night at 8 p.m., do not answer the phone every night. Call him in the morning and wish him a great day or text him for lunch. He should NOT be able to set his watch to your schedule. He should not expect to get some action every time he sees you. Make him wonder and pray that he will get it. This will keep him on his toes.

Rule #3: Lay the ground rules from the beginning.

It is your responsibility to teach him how to treat you. Make sure that you take the time now to write down your rules on paper so that when you are in the thick of your relationship, you don't go brain-dead and start making excuses for his poor behavior. Let me suggest some rules:

- No disrespecting you,
- No expecting sex before claiming you as his one-and-only,

- Absolutely no abuse and this includes grabbing your arms and pushing,
- No showing up late,
- No disappearing on you,
- No lying,
- No cheating,
- No keeping you from meeting his friends and family after you have been dating for at least six months.

Feel free to add the things that you absolutely will not tolerate and make sure that you stick to your principles. Men like women who have standards, but they don't need a mother either, so you can be firm without coming off as a nag (this is a major one Ladies, please pay attention to this one).

Rule #4: Keep dating at least two other guys until he commits to you.

Never close your options unless the guy you desire commits to date only you with the expectation of taking the relationship to the next level (i.e. marriage) in the near future. He should be the one to initiate this conversation because you are not eager or pressuring him to make you his girlfriend. You are simply enjoying yourself and going with the flow. Life is good, and you like the guy, but if things don't work out, you are okay because you have back pocket spares. If the dating period drags out past two months and he still hasn't mentioned his plans for you, let him go. Stop answering his calls, texts, or emails for at least one week. When you do finally answer his call, let him know you felt the relationship was not progressing and you don't have time to waste on anyone who doesn't know what he wants. Give him a chance to commit to you. He may have realized that he really does care about you and wants more from the relationship. If he does not make the move to elevate the relationship after your week-long disappearing act, cut him loose. He is just not that into you and doesn't deserve to be in the presence of a DIVA like you. It is important that you are just that cut and dry when dating. Too many women get caught up because they grow to really care for the man and allow him to string them along until he meets the woman he really wants. Do not allow any man to waste your time. Be disciplined and focus on what you truly want: A Life Partner!

Rule #5: When he goes through the rubber band phase, chill out and let him go.

Another advantage of dating more than two men at a time is that when he starts to pull away, you let him pull. You will not ask him, "What's wrong with you?" "Did I do anything wrong?" "Why won't you talk to me?" These questions are like the sound of Charlie Brown's teacher to a man ("Waunk, waunk, waunk"). Leave him be and give him space.

He will bounce back, but in the meantime, you have your attention occupied by your other dates.

Rule #6: Stay physically fit and love him like the relationship is new.

Make sure that your appearance stays top notch, that you continue to flirt with him, and that you continue to make your DIVA mark on him. Too many of you ladies let yourself go when you get a man. I shared in one of my *YouTube* videos (*www.youtube.com/lovein30days*) that I gained the 'love 15'. I actually gained 20 pounds in four months. It was ridiculous. However, I lost it all in three months. I explained in the video that studies have shown when two people enter a relationship or settle down in marriage, they often gain an average of at least 15 pounds. They attribute this sudden weight gain to having a partner to eat out with often, being distracted from pervious extracurricular activities, and having less time to exercise. Many feel a sense of comfort with eating all they want because they have found someone to love them.

I know that as a woman, keeping off weight can be difficult. We have babies, and our metabolism slows to a halt as we age, making it more difficult to drop those pounds. But I cannot emphasize enough that you must make an effort to stay physically fit – not only because you want to look your best for your man, but more

♥

importantly, so you can feel good about you. Most women who gain a significant amount of weight begin to feel worse about their looks, and this feeling of less confidence exudes an aura of insecurity. Insecurity is unattractive and a turn off. Please stop looking to your man to constantly affirm how attractive you are when you hate the way you look. This gets old and irritating to your man. Love yourself back to your desired size and keep the weight off.

Rule #7: Men love to have their egos massaged.

Tell him how great he is and praise him for his accomplishments. Men love to be recognized for the things that matter most to them. Let him know that you are in his corner and that you are paying attention by making him feel like a star when he earns it. Don't overdo this one. Some men will see through your attempt to win him over with fluffed-up praises. Remember that men like regular unleaded gas, not super premium. Gas his head up enough to make him feel great about himself but not so much so that he wonders if you really mean what you are saying.

Realistic Expectations

It always amazes me how many people enjoy trees and flowers, but they complain when it rains. In every relationship, being able to take the good with the bad is essential for long-term success. Today, when a couple experiences a little bit of challenge, they call it quits, hoping the next person will be better than the last. The problem is that you bring the same old you to a new situation. If you revert to your old way of limited thinking, then you may sabotage a new relationship and end up right back where you started. Yes, your ex could have been most of the problem, but you bear some of the blame for a bad relationship — even if it's merely the fact that you chose such a broken person.

Life will not be perfect just because you found your perfect partner. Do not have unrealistic expectations of what married life or a relationship will be like. Spending the rest of your life with your soulmate is one of the most rewarding joys on this side of heaven, but it does not come without its challenges. You must recognize that no matter how much you may have in common, you are coming together with different backgrounds, worldviews, and opinions. The key ingredients to any successful marriage, I discovered, are compromise and communication. If you focus on how to compromise, as well as communicate effectively with your spouse, you will have won half the battle. Don't believe the lies that most marriages end in divorce or with one or both partners living a life of suffering. If you choose the right person, and continue to grow and improve as a person, you will increase the chances of having a happy marriage.

The last major lesson that I learned as a married woman is that you cannot change anyone. Either you accept them as they are, or you move on. You will be moving on forever from one man to next if you are unwilling tolerate some annoying nuance about the other person. I am not telling you to stay with an abusing, lying, cheating fool just because you are determined to make it work. All of this is based on the understanding that you are marrying a good man and that you must both respect, honor, and treat each other right. A good marriage can easily slide down the slippery slope of unhappiness if you complain and focus on everything wrong with the other person. Remember the Law of Attraction? Whatever you focus on will become amplified. Whenever your spouse starts to get on your nerves, make a list of all his good traits and become thankful for those special qualities in your man. When everything about my husband started to irritate me, I got a love journal and started to write him a letter every day telling him how much I love and appreciate him and why. We have date night every week and I fall in love with him daily by paying attention to the great things he does for our family or to make me happy. We pray together daily and create yearly goals together. We are a team. There have been moments in time when we needed the guidance of our pastor in order to get back on track. Just like you would schedule a yearly physical with the doctor, we schedule yearly check ins with our pastor/counselor. We work at our marriage every single day and the reward is that I still get butterflies when he comes through the door or smiles at me. He is my best friend and business partner and I could not imagine life without him. I will write a book in the future about how to manifest a happy marriage.

Chapter 14.
Signs That He Is No Longer Feeling You

Sometimes relationships just don't work out, and we can do nothing about it. It isn't that you did something wrong – maybe he is an idiot and would not recognize a good thing if it fell directly on his head. This is not your problem, it is his. When you start to see the signs of a relationship's end, don't close your eyes and act as if you don't see them.

Men dread breaking up with women. You cannot blame them because we cry, beg, and act like pure fools. They would rather pull their eyes out than break up with you to your face, and as a result, they will begin to show signs that they are checking out long before they have actually checked out. Many men will wait until they have lined up another catch before breaking up with you.

When you start to see signs of the end, plan your exit strategy and break up with him first. Breaking up with him first will keep the ball in your court and be a lesser blow to your ego. Plus, he was the jerk who was acting up, why should he get the pleasure of ending things too? Keep your eyes open and trust your gut. If you feel things are going south, they probably are, but here are some sure signs that your relationship is heading down the drain.

Sign #1: He stops calling as much.

The phone is one of the best indicators of the status of your relationship. When he is feeling you, he will look forward to speaking to you daily. He will even call you throughout the day just to hear your voice. If he is calling once every other day or once a week or maybe even once a month, he is just not feeling you...enough. If you find yourself having to do most of the calling, stop calling him and see what happens with the relationship. See if he picks up the ball and starts calling. If the relationship dwindles into oblivion, therein lies your answer. He's just not really feeling you.

Sign #2: He stops asking you to go out with him or doesn't make an effort to spend time with you.

When a man is feeling you, he wants to spend as much time with you as possible and take you out from time to time. An indicator that the relationship is coming to an end is when he lives in the same state as you and is not the CEO of a Fortune 500 company or the President of the United States but has every excuse for why he is busy and doesn't have time to see you. Tell him to call you when he finds time on his schedule to make you a priority. Then put on your DIVA outfit with your sassy DIVA attitude and say "next." Get out of there and find someone else!

Sign #3: He is not willing to go out of his way for you.

If you have a flat tire in the middle of nowhere, and he says that he is busy, but you hear the TV and his boy yelling "touchdown," he is not really feeling you. When a man cares about you, he cares about your wellbeing and wants to be there for you during your times of need.

Sign #4: He'd rather hang out with the boys than hang out with you.

It is enough that he insults your intelligence by using the excuse that he is too busy with work as his reason why he has been seeing less and less of you. Now, with all of his activities, he still has time to go out with the guys! Is he gay? I think not! He is just not feeling you. I am not saying that you should spend all your waking hours in his presence, and I am not saying that he should not hang with his boys from time to time. I am just saying that if he is spending consecutive weekends with the boys and not making the same effort to hang with you, he is NOT, I repeat, not feeling you.

Sign #5: He only comes over when he is drunk and/or wants sex.

Lately your relationship has turned into a low-grade booty call. You two don't really spend time together, and you don't hear from him unless he is drunk and/or horny. He can't even express his emotions while he is sober. He has to confess his undying love for you while he is drunk. He doesn't respect you enough to come over once and awhile without wanting to get some. This is a red flag that he is not really feeling you.

Sign #6: He is caught lying to you.

It is not a good sign when he is lying about stupid things like having to work late when he's really at home watching the game. Or worse, he says that his cousin is coming to town and he will be a little busy showing her around town. In actuality, his cousin happens to be is his long-distance girlfriend who is in town for the weekend, so this is the reason you get his voice mail whenever you try to reach him. When he no longer cares about your feelings and can no longer be truthful with you, he is not feeling you. Love is kind, love is honest, and love feels good. Move on!

Sign #7: He doesn't even try to improve the things that he knows bother you, but instead, he does them even more.

When he demonstrates behaviors that hurt or significantly bother you, and you bring them to his attention, if, instead of making an effort to improve, his behavior just gets worse, he is pushing you away. Neither of you will ever be perfect, so you should be able to accept inconsequential traits that bother you. However, when you continually verbalize the same complaints, and there is no attempt to improve, he is not feeling you.

♥

Sign #8: He starts to accuse you of cheating when you have never given him any reason to suspect you.

When your man starts to act jealous and accuses you of wanting every man who walks by, it's because his lying butt is either cheating on you or thinking about it. In his mind, if he could be so slimy as to cheat, then you must be cheating on him too. This lessens his guilt and allows him to justify his behavior.

If your man is putting his little weed whacker in someone else, he is not really feeling you. This behavior is not only risky, but it is nasty as hell. He is bringing someone else's yuck yuck back to you! Just make sure that you are protecting yourself at all times, and do not stay with a man who is cheating on you.

Sign #9: He no longer asks you how your kids are doing.

When a man really cares about you, he will care about what matters most to you. If you two have dated for at least six months and he stops asking or doesn't ever ask about the most important people in your life, he is not really feeling you. Some men will avoid the children altogether out of guilt because they know they will be leaving the kid's life soon. Pay attention to the way he treats your kids or how interested he is in them. This one simple sign can tell you a lot.

Sign #10: He keeps his eyes closed lately whenever you have sex with him.

When the connection you used to share with him is no longer there, he is disconnecting himself from you. You will know what it feels like when he becomes disconnected because you will feel it in your gut as if he is somewhere else with someone else. Although you are participating in an act that is supposed to bring people closer, you will feel lonely and as if the love is no longer there. There is an exception to this one. It may be that he is busy, stressed out, or tired. You may need to talk about your concerns first before you kick him to the curb. However, if he is doing some of the other 'not feeling you' signs and he is disconnected during sex, then he is just not feeling you.

Sign #11: He brings out the worst in you.

When you are in love with your perfect partner, you will find yourself doing and becoming a better person. The One simply makes you want to do and be better in all areas of your life. When you are in a relationship that no longer serves you, you find that you are crying more often than laughing, yelling more often than talking, and complaining about life rather than living it to its fullest. When he no longer brings out the best in you, he is not feeling you.

Sign #12: If he is married or in a committed relationship with someone else.

As I stated in Chapter 6, a man with integrity would not be running around with you behind his wife's back while he claims he loves you. If he loves you so much and his marriage is falling apart, let him close that door first and prove that you are the one he desires. Everything else is just lip service, and he is not really feeling you.

DIVAs, striking out is part of the process of finding your perfect partner. If it isn't right, it isn't working, and one of you just isn't feeling the other one. Cut him loose and move on! There are so many wonderful things waiting for you when you find The One that it just isn't worth it to waste time on a relationship that isn't going to result in a long and happy marriage.

Chapter 15.
Sex Education for a DIVA

With the right chemistry, timing, and attitude, having sex becomes a bonus rather than the foundation of a relationship. Wisdom in this area is just as important as knowing how to attract the right man. You are learning how to be a sex goddess not for him but for yourself. I do not believe that it is acceptable to be an unsatisfied woman who simply focuses on pleasing her man. Sex is an important part of a committed long-term relationship and marriage. Make sure that you are pleasing your man and that your man is pleasing you.

The Sex Commandments

Here are the commandments about sex that have been handed down to me through experience and extensive investigation:

Commandment #1: Thou shall not have unprotected sex.

No explanation necessary. Keep condoms on hand and use them until you get married. NO need of dying or damaging your vajayjay because you were being ignorant and trusting a man because he appeared to be clean. There are men walking around with AIDS and you would never know it by looking at them. Be smart and play it safe.

Commandment #2: Thou shall not have sex without seeing his STD status within a 2-week period of your decision to make love.

This is a backup to Rule #1. You want to see his STD status even when you are practicing safe sex because, my friends, anything can happen. The condom can break, slip off, leak, or whatever. You can never be too cautious when it comes to your health. Even if he is clean, you still need to practice safe sex and use a condom. You still do not know if you are his only partner, and sometimes it takes AIDS three months to appear. (This is also Rule #4 in 'Avoid Getting Played' in Chapter 10.)

Commandment #3: Thou shall not have sex before marriage or without a commitment after having dated for at least 3 months.

You can do it. Just go to the sex shop and buy a great Jack Rabbit and go to work satisfying yourself for the next three months. Remember that the longer you wait, the more time you give him to see the qualities in you that will allow him to fall in love with you while he is chasing your goodies. No matter what men say about how they can have a one-night stand and fall in love with the woman, don't believe them. Men want to work for it. They are hunters by nature. They like sports for a reason. They love the challenge and the possibility that they may not get what they want. Do not rob them of this joy – when you give it up too soon, they wish in the back of their minds that you stopped them and made them wait. Moreover, sex will complicate things if a friendship has not developed first.

Commandment #4: Thou shall become his friend.

When you become his best friend, he is likely to fall in love with you and less likely to mistreat you. There is a disclaimer to this one, ladies: Do not tell the man you are with that you are waiting because you read in this book that you should wait three months before having sex with him. If he believes that the delay is deliberate and that you are waiting for any reason other than that you want to get to know him better or to make sure that you are making the right decision (which should be your motivation), he may wait long enough to get your goodies and drop you like a bad habit once he gets it. The men who I polled, 9 times out of 10, said that this would be a turn off and frustrate them. Also, remember the rules about not being 'friends-with-benefits'? Being his best friend and falling in love with each other is different from jumping in bed before a deep friendship is formed.

Commandment #5: Thou shall not have casual sex EVER!

Some women get so desperate to have a warm body next to them that they settle and have sex too soon with someone who does not deserve it. In addition to practical reasons, there is a scientific reason why a woman should wait before having sex and make sure he is the right guy. When a woman has sex with a man, she releases a chemical called Oxytocin. This is the same chemical, which is released when a woman has a baby, which causes a woman to bond with, nurture, and care for her child. If a woman is giving up the goods to the wrong guy, she becomes chemically addicted (or forms a soul tie) to a fool and wonders why she has such a hard time getting out of the negative situation.

Many women think that if men can have casual sex, they can do it too because it is a new day and time. This is not the case. How can God bring you your perfect partner when someone undeserving is occupying your mind, body, and heart? You must give up something in order to receive what you really want. You must be willing to be by yourself for a while in preparation to enjoy a lifetime with the one you want. Be patient, and he will come if you trust God and believe he will come.

Commandment #6: Thou shall not use your vagina as a currency.

I am surprised when I hear stories from men all over the country who explain how easy it is to get a woman to have sex with them. Many men make a sport of it and use it as bragging rights with their friends. Many women give up their vagina in the attempt to make a man fall for them and possibly take care of them. If you think you have liquid sunshine between your legs that can make a man fall head over heels in love with you, think again! If this were the case, prostitutes, strippers, and women who use their body for pay would be the most married group of women on the planet.

Everyone has an energy or aura. When a man enters a woman's body, he deposits his energy inside of her. Some of men are evil, perverts, cheaters, selfish, hateful, killers, addicts, or just plain crazy! After sex, a man can leave behind all of those negative energies within a woman's body, leaving her to deal with his issues. This is why it is a MUST that you get to know who you are sleeping with and choose him wisely. This is why selecting a man who has really submitted to God is the best man to select. This is why you must honor and love yourself by placing a real value on your body.

Commandment #7: Thou shall follow these rules if you do have sex too soon.

Now, for all my hot tamales, who ask, "What if I slip up and give him some before the three months are up?" First, it is better to wait, my little sex kittens, but if you slip up, you still have a shot to snag the man.

If you have sex with a man before the three months of dating, you MUST stick to these other dating rules to a T and keep dating at least two men at a time.

- Do not have sex with the others or him anymore.
- Do not sweat him, call, or text him before he has called or texted you at least twice prior.
- You must appear aloof as to where the relationship is going and how you feel about him.
- Work to create opportunities for you to spend quality time together so he is hooked on you, the person, to the point where if he lost you, his whole world would fall apart.

This is a very delicate tap dance, and we women naturally want to fall in love and lay it all on the line once we open our legs. The reason for this is because Mother Nature designed it this way. As I said previously, the Oxytocin hormone causes us to care deeply for the man we sleep with after about the fourth time you sleep together. Remember, you can still capture the heart of the man of your affection if there was already a connection, and you follow this advice. I have interviewed several men who have all admitted to falling in love with a woman after they started having sex within the first month of dating. This happened LESS often than the men who had to wait, but it did happen. Please understand that these stories are the exceptions, so do not hang your hat on this happening to you.

I was able to snag a guy after premature sex. I dated this guy with whom I had great chemistry, but at the time we met, I just knew I could never want anything serious with this man. I thought giving it up too soon wouldn't have any consequences because all I wanted was sex from him and nothing more. He chased me for about two months before we started speaking over the phone. When we started talking on the phone, I hardly ever called him. One day we hooked up, and I was hot in the pants and gave him some after only one month of dating. We continued to have sex, but I did not sweat him at all. I played it cool at all times, even when I began to develop feelings for him. We started to spend quality time together, and the more we learned about each other, the closer we grew and the better the sex. He eventually fell in love with me, and I did him. The sex, which initially was the primary part of our relationship, eventually became the cherry on top, and our friendship became primary, so much so that when we tried to break up, we could not stand the 24 hours apart. Prior to meeting my husband, I loved this man more than any man I had ever loved, and I believe that he felt the same for me. Please note that he would not ask me to marry him, so we eventually broke up. He was not The One for me, but he did help teach me how to create a deeply fulfilling relationship. The relationship started wrong, but if I had made the mistake that most women make and placed expectations on the relationship once we had sex by calling, texting, or revealing too much of my feelings up front, he would have run in the other direction and dropped me like a booty call.

♥

Commandment #8: Thou shall be upfront with him before you have sex if you have an STD.

It can be very embarrassing to have to tell your partner that you have herpes, AIDS, or any other sexually transmitted disease. This is the reason why it is important to wait at least three months before having sex with your partner. By the time you have sex together, you both should feel safe enough with the other person that you can share such an intimate detail about yourselves. It is only fair to share this piece of information with him, as you would hope he would share it with you.

Commandment #9: Thou shall not spend the night the first time you have sex with him.

Why, you ask? The reason you need to get yourself out of his bed the first time you have sex with him and go home is because you are continuing to confirm that you are a DIVA with a life and a sense of pride. You do not want to appear as the love-struck teenager who just lost her virginity. Sleeping underneath a man after sex will send the message that you are the type who may revolve your life around his, become clingy and/or needy. You have things to do in the morning, possibly kids to tend to, and errands to run. Give yourself space to contemplate how you really feel about the relationship.

Commandment #10: Thou shall not act as if you are a sexpert the first few times that you make love.

You may have been with more men than a madam and can do a backbend in the 69 position but keep this talent to yourself until the relationship grows a little bit stronger. You do not want him wondering where you learned this move and with how many men you've tried it. This is your business, not his. Keep him guessing and wondering by acting a little low key the first few times you are together. Work your way up to the master positions as you make him believe that he is the first one you are trying it out with.

♥

Commandment #11: Thou shall make him feel like he is the best you have ever been with, even if he is not.

Men have egos, and these egos are very sensitive. The top two questions in their mind after the first time of having sex with you are: did she enjoy me, and am I the best she has ever had? He really wants you to answer 'yes' to these questions — believe that! If you really care for him, make him feel that he is exceptional. Do not accept terrible sex. I am not advocating this. Just because he isn't as amazing as the man you used to travel to another galaxy with during sex, doesn't mean you cannot teach him how to please you. Sex may not be Earth shattering, but it should at least be satisfying.

Commandment #12: Thou shall not have sex with more than one man at a time.

Just because you are dating like a man does not mean that you need to have sex like one. Women are emotional, and when you have sex with more than one man, it increases the chances of generating confusion in your life. It increases the likelihood that you will be discovered and your reputation tainted, and it increases the chance of ending up on Maury having to figure out the answer to the question: "Who is the baby's daddy?"

Commandment #13: Thou shall not use sex as a bartering tool or a weapon.

Men hate when women withhold sex and use sex to get what they want, and they will grow to resent you if you do this to them too often. Not having sex occasionally because you are tired and do not feel like it is acceptable. Offering him sex in exchange for taking out the trash, for instance, is a habit that you do not want to start. This takes the sacredness and joy out of sex and turns it into a task.

Commandment #14: Thou shall not talk about marriage, having kids together, or meeting the parents after the first lovemaking session. Just don't do it. He will tell you how good it was and never call again because you have scared the man into thinking that you are too clingy.

What Men Like

It is no secret that men love sex more than food, football, and free parking. To illustrate the importance of sex for men, get a number in your head, multiply it by a billion, take that number to the depths of the earth, multiply this number by infinity, and you still come nowhere close to how much a man enjoys great sex. I recommend buying a copy of *The Kama Sutra* and explore the world of Tantric sex. *The Kama Sutra* is a book of various sexual positions from ancient India. It is the most advanced guide to sexual positions in history. Tantric sex explores a deeper connection during sex. Expertise in the Kama Sutra teachings and Tantric sex will take your love and lovemaking to a level beyond anything than you could possibly imagine. Sex will be more fulfilling and gratifying when you have a greater understanding of the act. In addition, when you make love the right way with the one you truly love, you will visit planets and galaxies that you never thought existed.

Please note that this next sex section s for married people ONLY or seriously committed people. I am not attempting to train a new breed of freaks. I am simply arming you with information you will eventually need when you meet your perfect partner. I understand that not all of you will wait until marriage, but at least wait until you are in love, committed, and moving toward marriage. Let's explore some specifics most men enjoy:

Men like good oral sex

They write books about it, talk about it in comedy shows, and daydream about it as they talk about it with their friends. Men love great fellatio. They will do anything to get great oral sex. By the same token, they will cut you off the potential list if you can't figure out how to do it well. If you need to practice on a dildo, please do so.

Make sure that you cover your teeth with your lips. Men do not want you playing around down there and scraping your teeth against their penis. Make sure that you lick the outside of the penis first, before you start. Make sure that you use lots of saliva. Start slow and make sure that your mouth is really wet. The deeper you can go the better. Pretend you have the world's greatest lollipop in your mouth. If you aim the penis towards the roof of your mouth, then you are less likely to gag when it goes down your throat. Place your hand around the shaft and jack it off as you move you hand in sync with your mouth. Get faster and make sure that you focus on the tip of the penis. Most of the nerve endings are in the tip, so this is the most sensitive part of the penis. If you can swallow without biting his penis as you move up the shaft, then he will go crazy!

If you do not want him to come in your mouth, which you shouldn't until he marries you, take your thumb and press it at the base of the penis on the inside, where that big vein meets his body. Press it lightly but firmly enough to keep his cum from erupting into your mouth. Give him oral sex long enough for him to either climax or pull you up to him so that he can finish the session by pleasing you with his penis inside of you or returning the favor by going down on you.

Learn this craft well and do whatever it takes to get over your inhibitions if you are one of the many women out there who do not like going down on her man. Many Christian women have problems giving their husbands oral sex. My advice is to get over it. Nothing in the Bible says that you cannot please your husband in any way necessary, as long as it does not involve animals, sharp objects or other people. I hate to say it, but good fellatio is so important that men say that they can love their wife but may cheat on her in order to get good oral sex. Take, for example, Bill Clinton. He risked his career, self-respect, and marriage for good fellatio. I did not make the rules; I just understand them and proceed to advise accordingly.

Again, please understand that this advice is more for the married folks or people who are in long-term committed relationships. Do not give this gift to every man you meet, date or like.

Men enjoy quickies.

Most women prefer romantic love making to a quickie. This is understandable, and you do not want a sexual experience based solely on quickies. However, quickies can be fun and necessary for both parties, especially when time is limited. Be flexible and give your man a quickie if you are, for example, at a friend's house and need to run to the bathroom for a quick fix; if you are late for work but want to start the day off right; or you are in an elevator and would like to spice things up. (Be careful, I do believe they have cameras in most elevators.) Whatever the reason or location, try to make quickies a part of your sexual routine. Men like when you can let go and get freaky with them. If you have not learned by now, I will share a secret with you. All men, I repeat, all men want a good girl out in public during the day and a freak in the bedroom at night. When you have snagged the perfect partner for you, become his ultimate fantasy, and do whatever it takes to please him. Be willing to try new things. You might just enjoy and learn something new in the process about your own sexual desires.

Men like to hear their names called during sex.

When you say a man's name during lovemaking, it does something to their ego. It's like a shot of morphine, as it gives him a high when he has recognized he is the one who can make your experience so pleasurable. You can say it loudly or softly, but just say their names, and they will continue to attempt to do whatever it takes to keep you saying their names.

Men like it when you lift their legs and lick between their anus and testicles.

I am not a man, so I am not sure why, but I have received reports from many men who say there is a sensitive area between the testicles and the anus called the 'taint' that if stimulated correctly, will drive a man crazy in ecstasy. I suggest you take this one slowly the first time you do it and be aware that to some men, having their legs lifted in the air may make them feel a bit homosexual. If you do it right and maybe lick around the area while their legs are still down, and slowly work to lift their legs up in the air as you gain approval — they will be moaning, trust me — they will become more receptive as they experience the pleasure.

Men like it from the back.

I have been scratching my head as to why men like to give it from the back so much. I guess it doesn't matter. They like it, so just give it to them. It is more fun when he leads, flips you over, and puts you in the doggystyle position. Let him initiate this position most of the time.

Men like to hear that they have the biggest 'third leg' that you have ever had.

I know, he doesn't have the biggest one that you have ever had but tell him he does anyway. You know how to do this because we do it all the time when a child draws us an unrecognizable picture or our boss ask us for our opinion and we tell them what they want to hear. When your child comes smiling from ear to ear proudly presenting his or her masterpiece, naturally you tell your child that it is the best thing that you have ever seen in your life. You say it with so much conviction that the child actually believes it and continues to draw pictures that can be showcased on the refrigerator.

The size of a man's anatomy has to be his biggest source of insecurity or pride depending on the size. Help improve his self-esteem by letting him know how much you enjoy his penis and telling him what he needs to hear in order to be the sexual warrior he needs to be in the bedroom. Sometimes, if you have a man who is deficient in penis size, you will have to use your feminine charm to convince him that it's not the size of the boat that matters, but the motion in the ocean. Let him know that he turns you on by the way he looks at you, touches you, holds you, and loves you.

If you are truly attracted to him and turned on by him, he will feel and know your sincerity. If you are not attracted, sexually pleased or turned on by him, you will need to get a new boat for your ocean.

As mentioned previously, it is very important that you and your man are compatible: emotionally, spiritually, mentally, and physically. Compatibility is a must, or the love will go out the window when the going gets tough. There are exceptions, but this is more a rule than an exception. A penis that might be too small and unsatisfying for you may be very pleasing to someone else and vice versa. Love yourself enough to get what you need or deserve.

Men love to make their women climax.

Some women have a difficult time climaxing. We take a lot longer than a man to come, for the most part, and we must be mentally stimulated in order to reach an orgasm. To remedy the possibility of disappointing their man, women have developed a universal habit of faking an orgasm. Sometimes the sex feels great, but for whatever reason, you cannot come. Because you do not want your man working overtime in futile disappointment trying to get you to climax, you fake it to save his ego and your vagina. This is okay, as long as you don't make it a habit.

You should learn what it takes to get you to orgasm so that you can share that experience with your mate, and sex can become a fulfilling experience for both of you. You can experiment with dildos and vibrators, but I suggest that you get your mind on the orgasm page. The physical stimulation that leads to an orgasm is only a small fraction of the requirements to get a woman to peak sexually. A woman's biggest sex organ is between her ears (her brain), so figure out what you must experience mentally in order to come. Do you need to experience complete trust with you man? Do you need him to talk to you during sex? Do you need to imagine Idris Elba making love to you? What will it take to turn you on mentally to get you to come? Once you figure this out, experiencing an orgasm will become a breeze. In fact, you will begin to experience multiple orgasms, and this is when the real fun begins.

Men like to wonder if they will get sex.

Men want to want you. Do not give him some at his discretion. Give him some at your discretion. Sometimes say no, you are tired, busy, on your period, or whatever. They will appreciate it more the next time you give them some. Try not to turn them down too much because balance is the key.

Men enjoy being stroked.

Rub your hands through their hair, touch their face, and whisper sweet nothings in their ears as they are making love to you. Affectionately touch them at random times for no reason. The gesture will go a long way.

Men like to be told what they can do to please you.

Be open about your desires in the bedroom. If you do not tell him what you like, he will never know. No two women are the same, so if you leave it up to him, he will do what pleased the last woman he was with, and it might not be the same as your pleasures. Leave shyness at the door when you enter the bedroom and let him know what you like sensually.

Break your old soul ties before you enter a new relationship.

When a woman finds it difficult to walk away from a relationship with a man who does not treat her right and she knows that she should leave, she has formed a soul tie with the wrong man. A soul tie is an intense spiritual bond with another person whom you have allowed to sexually enter your body. In our culture, sex has been trivialized and relegated to being merely a physical act, but in reality, it is a spiritual act as well.

When another person enters your body, your spirits are merging as one. This impacts women more than men because women's sex organs are internal. A woman may feel stuck because she can't stop thinking about or wanting the man who has broken her heart more times than she can count. Many women report to me that it feels like having an out-of-body experience where she is standing outside of herself and cannot stop herself from making stupid decisions as it relates to the wrong guy.

A victim of rape who has not done the healing work I discussed earlier will most likely have soul ties that may cause her to have a block at the door of her vagina that makes it darn near impossible for her to be intimate with someone else. Intimacy is more than physical. It is allowing someone to connect with you emotionally on the deepest level.

The good news is that there is a way to break a soul tie quickly and permanently. I offer this to my coaching clients who desperately want to be free of spiritual bondage to the wrong man. Listen to the "Breaking Soul Ties" meditation for 30 days. Call me for coaching if you need it. I will help you heal on a spiritual level that will begin the process of permanent healing. The idea is that no matter where you go for help or what you do to disconnect the cord that keeps you connected to the man who is wrong for you, it is imperative that this cord be cut before attempting to enter a healthy relationship with a different man.

Sex is a very important part of any seriously committed relationship. I have created this chapter because many women are insecure in the bedroom because they are afraid of their inability to please a man and because they lack the expectation that they should also be pleased. I do not want this to stand in your way. In a seriously committed relationship, sex should be free, fun, and fully satisfying. Master the lessons taught in this chapter and read other sexual mastery books that incorporates sex and spirituality. I promise you that you have never experienced anything more amazing than the Tao of Lovemaking. Open your mind and learn about this awesome experience while using the wisdom of selectivity. Not everyone deserves this level of connection with you. Be selective!

Chapter 16.
Creating Healthy, Promising Relationships

Now you have gotten the man who seems to be The One for you, and you desire to ensure that you have a successful long-term relationship that leads to marriage. How do you keep the music playing, so to speak? Here are some rules to remember to establish and maintain a healthy promising relationship:

What Not to Do While in a Relationship

Do not talk about the ex all the time or compare him to your ex.

He may ask. He may act as if he is interested and wants to know every detail of your past relationships but resist the temptation to overload him with talk of your exes. If you tell him how your ex bought you special gifts, then he will start to compare himself even without you doing it. If he doesn't give you gifts as often, he will start to feel less significant in your life. If you tell him how your ex slapped your butt during sex, he may feel inadequate about himself or you. Just don't create this kind of negativity in your life. Leave the past in the past.

Do not cry in front of him often or be a drama queen.

Men don't like or respect weak, needy women. These kinds of women scare them because a man won't know what to do to make his woman feel better. If a man cannot save the day and make you feel better, he will feel insignificant and start to disconnect from you.

Don't act as if you are a man or a superhero who is strong all the time under all situations.

Let the man be the man and trust him after he earns your trust. You have been giving so much of yourself to your children, your job, your family, and friends, but now it is time to allow someone to give to you. Let go, love with your whole heart, and cry on his shoulder when you feel at your lowest. Remember, he should have passed all your tests, had most of the characteristics on your perfect partner list, and opened himself to you before you give him your trust. Being vulnerable with a man who has earned your trust and respect is the only way you will experience true love.

Do not allow him to believe that you cannot live without him or your whole life revolves around him.

He should feel that if he screwed up badly (i.e. cheating constantly, lying, putting his hands on you, etc.), you would have no problem kicking him to the curb. Be careful not to use your ability to leave as a weapon you hang over his head. You should be subtle in sending this message, and if he really cares about you, he will think twice before doing something to screw things up. You should also have too much of a life to be at his disposal whenever he needs you. Let him miss you. A woman who is always available is a boring woman indeed. Get a life, and he will have something to look forward to and brag about to all his friends.

Do not call him more than once to every two times he calls you.

The goal is to be the deer, not the hunter, even at this stage. The phone is a measure of how much he cares about you. Allow him to show you that he cares. Give him a chance to miss you and allow him to work his butt off for you because you are worth it. You are the golden ring, the trophy and the prized possession. Let him use his #1 weapon, the phone, as part of his method to win you over and keep you.

Do not try to change him.

Maya Angelou said, "When someone shows you who they are, believe them." You must listen to who he is and not try to make him who you want him to be. You cannot change anyone but you, and that is difficult enough. If you are dissatisfied with him or he demonstrates any of your non-negotiable traits, then he is not The One for you.

Do not nag him.

Men dread being nagged. After too much nagging, he will shut down, and your words will turn into noise to him. If you have something that you need to address with him, talk to him when the mood is right, when you are both relaxed, and he is paying attention. Use the subconscious conditioning method I discussed in Chapter #13 in the Realistic Expectations section.

There will never be a perfect man, so make a list of his bad traits and pick the top two that you know you refuse to live with, and only focus on improving those traits. If you have a good man — you should if you followed this manual — you must be willing to take some bad with the good. Choose your battles, and don't harp on everything he does wrong.

Do not talk negatively about his mother.

The type of man who you want is the kind who loves his mother. It will not reflect favorably on you if you are talking negatively about his mother even if she is a real piece of work. Going off on the mother is a first-class ticket to a breakup, so no matter what she says or does to you, it is his job, not yours, to stand up to his mother. If he is not standing up to her on your behalf, take this as a flashing neon sign that he is just not feeling you or not man enough for you, and move on.

Do not be overly jealous or accuse him of cheating.

Many women are healing from betrayal in their past, and this creates a level of distrust for every other man who comes into their lives after the hurt. Just because you are still working on your insecurities, projecting those fears onto your potential perfect partner is unfair.

Warning: if your instincts are telling you that something is up, find solid evidence before you start accusing him. Make sure that you have valid proof before you start to accuse him of cheating, or you may push a man to cheat or leave when he was never thinking of doing either.

Do not allow your best friend and your man to hang out by themselves.

If you leave the house, one of them should be leaving with you. Never let your friends play near your cookie jar. Trust your man and watch your friends. You may not know that your friend envies your relationship and deep-down desires what you have. One day she may become weak and decide to slip and fall on your man's stuff. I know, I know, your man or friend would never do this to you. Well, that is exactly what the other women who have had it done to them said before it happened to them. Prevent this from happening, and just don't allow the atmosphere to begin.

Do not make him feel bad for looking at an attractive woman when she walks within eyeshot.

Most men notice an attractive woman in half the time it takes us to notice. Most of them would rather pluck their eyes out than get caught by you looking at another woman. Be different, make a positive comment about her features. In fact, tell him to look at that attractive girl. This will throw him off, and he will start to see you as more than his girlfriend, he will begin to see you as his best friend. This will demonstrate that you are a confident DIVA, and he will store in the back of his mind that he can be honest with you on other subjects. I am not suggesting you allow him to disrespect you. He should be mature enough to catch a glance and keep it moving. Make sure that you set healthy boundaries and leave room for him to be a man around you.

❤

Do not prostitute your love.

Yes, I know that this sounds like a crazy statement, but I need your attention. Most people do not know how to truly love someone. This is the reason why couples start off madly in love one day and hating each other the next. I truly believe that if more people learned how to give the gift of unconditional love, less turmoil would exist in relationships today. Love has four levels: Level 1, Level 2, Level 3, and God's Love.

Level 1 Love is referred to as selfish, infancy love. The best example is that of an infant. The baby wants what it wants. You feed it, change it, wash it and cuddle it, and it will take all the love you give it. An infant has no concept of love, so it continues to receive without any effort to give love back. Level 1 love takes without giving back. It is all about you and no one else. It is safe to love at level 1 because you are safe from being hurt. You never allow anyone to penetrate your hard shell because becoming vulnerable is your greatest fear, and you just refuse to be hurt again. Loving at level 1 is like a boat that never leaves the dock. Yes, it is safe at shore, but the boat was never created to stay at shore.

Level 2 Love is what I like to refer to as prostituting your love. In this level you say, "I will only love you as long as you love me back the way I want you to love me." At this love level, like a prostitute, love is given like a currency only when there is an even exchange. The moment the other person stops loving in the manner they desire, treating their beloved with adoration or giving to them in a manner that they expect, the love is removed. The love may even turn into hate with no trace that the love ever existed in the first place.

Level 3 Love is where the magic begins. At this level, you choose to love with no restrictions, demands or expectations. A sense of freedom opens to you because at this level, you have made the conscious decision to love someone else even if they do not return that love the way you think they should. You simply love them, and in loving them, you receive the gift you also give them — freedom and unconditional acceptance. I am not saying to love a fool and let him take advantage of you. I have already shared with you what type of man you should select. The potentially right man is a man who has already submitted to God and who is most of what is listed on your perfect partner list. When you love at level 3 and you release this person, you are not angry or bitter toward anyone but, instead, grateful for the opportunity to experience this level of loving. You understand that even if it doesn't work out with him, the love you gave to him is just practice for the man who is truly meant for you. The most interesting outcome of loving someone at this level is that it only takes one of you to decide to love without demands, restrictions or expectations. What happens, more often than not, is that the other person drops his or her guard and begins to love unselfishly, too. It is amazing and magical. This love never ends even if the relationship does. It offers the peace to move on and love another without resentment and old baggage.

God's Love is simply God's love and cannot be outdone. It is amazing to know that God loves me no matter what I have done, thought, or said, and that nothing I can do will remove God's love from me. Knowing this helps me to remember that I am not doing anyone any favors by loving them at Level 3. We are all capable of loving someone without out any demands, restrictions or expectations because God loves us like this. Don't get me preaching up in here!

Many people tell me that this kind of love does not exist and that loving someone with no expectations can lead to extreme heartbreak. I always answer by saying: First, Level 3 love does exist, and anyone can love at this level. Second, if you are touring the Empire State Building and fall off the 13th or 33rd floor, both falls would hurt! Do not shortchange your love experience because you are afraid of what could happen. Moreover, the view on the 33rd floor is so much better! Remember, with great risks come great rewards. Like the boat, you were not designed to give mediocre love. You were created to love as God loves. This is the only way to experience pure love, and this is why we were all created.

Never stop learning how to become a better you.

Although I do believe that this book is the most comprehensive dating and relationship guide on the market today, I also believe that it is important for every woman to become a student of love. You can never know too much. The reason I was able to avoid severe heartbreak and acquire the ability to size up a man in five minutes and kick him to the curb if I detected he wasn't worthy is because I studied men, the art of dating, and the patterns of love. Several very good books are out there that can assist you in understanding men and offer effective ways of communicating with them.

Most women understand that men and women speak different languages. When you learn what a man is trying to say, you can respond in a way that makes him feel understood. Even as 'The Love DIVA', I continue to study and learn all I can about how to have a successful relationship. I have been married and divorced from other people and my husband has never been married before. We have both witnessed dysfunctional relationships in our parent's lives and want to create a better example for our children. We both declared, "Divorce is not an option for us!" In our minds, the only option we have is to make it work. Although we spent lots of time and money on our wedding, we spent as much, if not more, time on preparing to have a successful marriage by going to premarital counseling. I read lots of books to increase my level of understanding about men, how to have a successful marriage and how to align my thoughts and expectations with what I want to manifest in life. You should never stop being willing to learn. After you read my book, pick up books by John Gray, Steve Harvey, and T.D. Jakes. Read this book two more times and keep it on your nightstand as a reference guide when you have doubts or uncertainty in your love life. Maya Angelou said it best, "When you know better, you do better!" Continue to learn more, so that you can attract and experience better.

Avoid moving in with him before marriage.

We live in an era when more couples are cohabiting before marriage. Cohabitation was once rare, but researchers have found that more than half (54 percent) of all first marriages begin with cohabitation. Statistics further suggest that a majority of men and women of marriageable age today will spend some time cohabiting prior to marriage.

While popular, cohabitation is less stable than marriage. Here are some statistics showing why moving in with your boyfriend is probably not a good idea:

- Living together is thought to be more stressful than being married.
- Just over 50 percent of cohabiting couples ever get married.
- 57 percent of cohabiting couples dissolve within ten years when compared with 30 percent of all first marriages (VanGoethem 2005).
- In the United States and in the UK, couples that live together are at a greater risk for breaking up than non-cohabiting couples.
- Couples who lived together before marriage tend to divorce early in their marriage. If their marriage lasts seven years, then their risk for divorce is the same as couples who didn't cohabit before marriage.
- Cohabiting couples have a rate of separation that is five times that of married couples, and, in the event of separation, cohabitors have a rate of reconciliation that is only 33 percent as high as that of married couples (Binstock 2003).
- The U.S. Justice Department found that women are 62 times more likely to be assaulted by a live-in boyfriend than by a husband (Colson 1995).
- Cohabiting women have rates of depression three times higher than married women (National Institute for Mental Health).

Men respect titles so do not ever allow a man to refer to you as 'wifey,' or another casual variation of 'wife,' as you assume the role of his wife without him having to make a major commitment. I have known women who lived with their boyfriends for more than seven years, cooking and cleaning, and taking care of him only to never get a marriage proposal. Fed up and tired of waiting, these women come running to me asking why their live-in boyfriends will not marry them. The answer is simple. The men will not marry these women because they do not have to marry them to get what they want. Ironically, some of these former long-term, live-in boyfriends end up getting married after dating some other woman for only two months.

You are a DIVA who comes with a high stock value. You do not give away your mind, heart and body to a man who feels that you are only good enough to live with but not good enough to marry. Having standards that you will not deviate from no matter what, is important in attracting and sustaining a healthy relationship.

What Not to Reveal Until after the Wedding

Out of all of my videos on *YouTube*, the video on "The Top 5 Things to Never Tell Your Man" is probably the video men hate most. They feel that I am suggesting for a woman to lie to her man or not be upfront. I advocate withholding certain information because a man will declare that he wants to know everything about the woman he is dating, and what she says will not affect his opinion of her. Many women fall for this lie, but I am telling you that you should keep some things to yourself. I am not saying to be something that you are not. If you are a call girl by night and a librarian by day, I do believe that who you are will eventually come out. I am saying that most women, if not all women, have a past, and many are too eager to share their entire past with the man they like or love. Men are visual, and once they form an image about you, erasing that image from their heads is very difficult.

I do not believe that your man should know EVERYTHING about your past because your past does not necessarily dictate your future and likely has little to do with who you are today. Do not allow a man to make you feel less than who you are because of what you have done in your past. Learn from your past, pray about it and keep it between you and the Lord. Keep the following information to yourself:

That you had a threesome in college or that your secret fantasy is to have a threesome.

Although every man in the world has probably fantasized about being involved in a threesome, they do not welcome their future wife to have been involved in a threesome. I know it's a double standard. Get over it. It is what it is, and good men lose respect for women who have participated in activities such as this. Your past is nothing to be ashamed of, and you should not hold your head down because of a fantasy. Just keep it to yourself, and only talk about it with the girls.

That you have been treated poorly by guys all of your life.

Up until your perfect partner marries you, you will speak positively about all of your exes and simply say that the relationship ended because things just didn't work out. You do not want to create the image in his head that it is okay for him to mistreat you. If every man has hurt you, he will wonder what is wrong with you to have attracted these types of men. In addition, if you are constantly harping on what happened in the past, you will continue to attract that experience into your life.

That you have cheated in the past.

I recommend that you keep this one to yourself, and make sure that this is a habit you break forever. You do not want him wondering if you would do the same thing to him.

♥

That you have had more than seven sex partners and have gone down on more than three.

This is another one you need to take to your grave. Men need to think of their women as pure and innocent, the cream of the crop. Knowing that you have been with the baseball team in college will throw you off the pedestal on which he has placed you. Men just cannot handle imagining more than seven men making love with their woman.

That you were a stripper while in college to pay your way through school or to feed the kids.

Trust me on this one, the pole expertise will not impress him, and he will not follow through on his promise not to judge you because of your past. Keep it to yourself forever!

That you had an eating disorder, a mental breakdown, or see ghosts.

We all have our hang-ups and life issues. Life's challenges are designed to make you stronger and grow as a person and are not to be broadcasted as a shadow of your past. The ability to see ghost is a gift that many have but not all understand. Use discernment when sharing taboo gifts such as seeing the dead. If seeing or communicating with the dead cause you pain or distress, let it go and choose a different experience. Let the dead bury their dead, and never speak about it again. Simply focus on the bright future ahead of you, free of all memories of your past challenges. Continue to get therapy for these issues if necessary. Make sure that you are actively attempting to heal them. If you must share these intimate details of your life, wait until you are deeply in love or married, and he is committed to loving and cherishing you until death do you part. That way, he won't head for the hills when you tell him about the minor issues that you faced in your past.

💙

That you see a therapist for your issues.

Again, most people need to see a shrink but do not because of society's stigma on mental health. Seeing someone to discuss and help handle your problems is something about which you should not be ashamed. Actually, seeking professional help takes a high level of courage. Broadcasting it on Jerry Springer is another matter altogether. Let your man grow to love you for your strengths and allow your wounds to heal themselves. If you must tell him, allow him to grow to love you first before you do so.

That you bite your toenails

This is nasty, by the way, but some of you do it. Just don't let him catch you doing this, or it may affect his ability to get it up the next time you want sex after he has seen your mouth on your toes.

That you have an insurance policy that is paid to your husband in the event of your untimely death.

This is another one that should probably be kept to yourself until you two have been married for at least 10 years. He doesn't need any temptations while love is taking root. You do not need to worry in the back of your head that if things go wrong, he will go psycho on you, kill you, leave the bloody glove as evidence, be exonerated, and take your trust fund and insurance policies.

That you have freaky sex secrets that you have done to past sex partners.

Again, you want your man to think highly of you at all times. Your past does not determine who you are today, but sometimes men can and will hold it against you. Do you really believe that he is going to tell you all of his freaky sex secrets? I think not! Let's learn from men and keep our mouths shut about our dirty little secrets.

That your family on your father's side is crazy as hell,
drink like sailors, and fight at funerals.

Do I really need to say anything else about this? Everyone has
someone in their family whose behavior is embarrassing. You are
not the people in your family. If most of your family members are
crazy but it has not negatively influenced you, what is the point of
discussing them in the beginning of a relationship? If you stay
together, he will eventually discover these things for himself, but
you don't need to scare him by telling him all about the
unappealing side of your family before he has even had a chance to
fall in love with you.

Ladies, I am not advocating dishonesty with this list. I am merely
advising you to keep your past in the past. There are some things
that you should discuss, like the fact that you have been married
before, or that you have children. But we are all human and have
made mistakes that really don't need to follow us around as we
work to build a better life.

Chapter 17.
Keep the Ball Rolling

Sometimes finding the love of your life is a numbers game, and you must act accordingly. Many of the dates that you go on will be disappointing, and the men you meet won't even make it past "hello," but don't give up. Like the old saying goes, you must kiss a few toads to find your prince. Just think of it like anything else you ever accomplished that was worth having. Did you give up job hunting when you were turned down for a position you wanted? What about those shoes you wanted so badly that weren't in your size, so you traveled to the mall across town that had them in stock. If you can hang in there after those simple life challenges, surely you can stick in there until you find your perfect partner.

You have to make up your mind that quitting is not an option, and you will not stop accepting dates until you find The One. Whatever you do, do not settle. If he does not meet your needs or he is a great guy, but you just do not feel 'it' for him, let it go and find someone who will make your heart sing. When you find The One, you will look forward to every tomorrow because you know that you have found your best friend and your divine mate. He is out there looking for you just as you are looking for him. When you start to get discouraged, remind yourself of this fact and believe it with everything in you, and I guarantee you, he will show up.

Enjoying the Process

As you are dating and open to finding your life partner, remember to have fun. This process is not a job, race, or a destination, it is a journey. It is this journey that prepares you for the wonderful experience of finding your perfect mate. You must stay focused on your goal and enjoy the process along the way. Do not be one of those women who dines with the friends or sits at the bar complaining to any and everyone who will listen to their hate for the opposite sex and dating challenges. The more you dread it, the more you will attract dreadful experiences into your dating experience. Take it lightly, make mistakes, learn as you go, pay attention, and listen to your gut. The more you flow smoothly through this process, the easier it will get, and the stronger your confidence will grow. You will start to develop an air about you that radiates the message "I deserve the best, and I will not settle until I find it." It is this magnetic light that will attract the type of man you desire into your life.

The DIVA Motto

Repeat this motto aloud:

"I am a sexy, sassy DIVA. I will date more than one man at a time without guilt. Whenever I walk into a room, heads will turn because I am a man magnet, and my essence radiates so brightly, that everyone wants to know who I am. I will respect myself enough to allow the man to work hard for my affection as he demonstrates that he is my perfect partner. In the event I accidentally chose a perfect loser as my perfect partner, I will discard him immediately and move on to date until my true divinely selected perfect partner finds me."

In Closing

The world of dating can be fun if you are armed with the right attitude, expectations and outlook. Like everything else in life, there are laws to dating that we must adhere to if we are to be happy and find The One person that is out there for each and every one of us. As you master an understanding of how men think and then proceed wisely through the world of dating, finding a man will become a simpler undertaking. Be patient with yourself if you mess up after not adhering to the suggestions in this book. Simply know that you are a work in progress and that the next time you will do better. The funny thing is that what will most likely happen is that you will eventually reach a 'wholeness' within you and without even looking, you will meet The One. Things will click without the necessity of rules and you will just know that you are finally home. This will not happen over a day, a few weeks, or even months. You won't rush the process because you will trust the process. You won't have to resist, think too hard, or remember what to do or say because things will just flow. Follow the rules in this book until this magical moment happens. Have fun and be blessed as you move forward into finding that perfect man for you. I love you all and wish the blessing of true, unconditional love upon you.

Affirmations

Affirmations work best when said repeatedly with emotional intensity.

Must say the 1st week of your journey:

> I love you (say your name).

Must say the 2nd week of your journey:

> I am open and receptive to receive and give love.

Must say the 3rd week of your journey:

> My husband is on his way to me now!

Must say the 4th week of your journey:

> True love flows in and through me as me.

Must say the 5th week of your journey:

> My past does not equal my future. A great relationship flows to me now!

Must say the 6th week of your journey:

> I am strong, vulnerable, and loving in my relationships.

Must say the 7th week of your journey:

> I am now divinely irresistible to my perfect partner.

After the 7 weeks, pick your top five favorite affirmations below and repeat until your soulmate comes into your life. Do not lose faith no matter how things may look.

Must say in your head whenever you are out in public:

> I am a radiant DIVA and every man in the room wants to be with me!

> I am a man magnet and I draw my perfect partner to me now!

> My perfect partner is on his way to me now!

> I am comfortable around men and do not have to try too hard to earn their love. I am good enough the way I am.

> Love happens! I release the desperate need for love. I release the need for my partner to approve of me. I allow love to find me easily and effortlessly.

> The more I love myself, the more I attract love.

> I am surrounded by love. All is well.

> I am feminine and full of grace.

> I love myself and I naturally attract loving relationships into my life.

> I am now attracting exactly the kind of relationship I want and deserve.

> I release excessive control. I know that I will be able to recognize my perfect partner and be vulnerable to him.

> My partner is loyal to me.

> There are plenty of great men, and one is on his way to me now.

> I know that my soul mates waits for me as I wait for him.

> I will not settle for less than I deserve, nor will I have unrealistic expectations.

References

Bachman, Ronet (1994). *Violence Against Women: A National Crime Victimization Survey Report*. Washington, DC: Bureau of Justice Statistics. p. 6.

Binstock, G. and Thornton, A. (2003). Separations, reconciliations, and living apart in cohabiting and marital unions. *Journal of Marriage and Family*. 65(2):432-443.

Colson, Charles (1995). As quoted in "Five reasons you need the 'Piece of Paper'". *Focus on the Family*, 2000.

Gray, John (1992). *Men are from Mars, Women are from Venus*. New York, NY: Harper Collins.

Kamp Duch, Claire, Cohan, M. Catherine L., and Amato, Paul R. (2003)."The Relationship Between Cohabitation and Marital Quality and Stability: Change Across Cohorts?" *Journal of Marriage and Family*. Vol. 65, August 2003. pp. 539-549.

Manning, Wendy D. (1993). "Marriage and Cohabitation Following Premarital Conception." *Journal of Marriage and the Family* 55:839-850.

Marazziti, Donatella and Canale, Domenico (2004). "Hormonal changes when falling in love: *Psychoneuroendrocrinology*, 29, 921-936.

Rindfuss, A., and VanDenHeuvel, A. (1990). "Cohabitation: A Precursor to Marriage or an Alternative to Being Single?" *Population and Development Review* 16:703- 726.

Robbins, Anthony. (1996). *Personal Power*. Niles, IL: Nightingale Conant Corp.

Stets, Jan E. (1991). "Cohabiting and Marital Aggression: The Role of Social Isolation." *Journal of Marriage and the Family* 53:669-680. One study found that, of the violence toward women that is committed by intimates and relatives, 42% involves a close friend or partner whereas only 29% involves a current spouse.

Visit the author's web page to get more information on her upcoming books, TV appearances, radio interviews, and other engagements: www.ShayBetter.com,
or go to www.BlackBettyBoopShop.com to purchase high vibration products.